Front cover: Jet Provost Mk 5 circa 1985 from RAF Linton On Ouse, photographed by the author

Thanks to Jess for help, Pip for inspiration and my parents for their encouragement.

D1494752

Chapter 1

Not the same as a Cessna

The Sundays dragged; mainly because on Saturday I blew my wages and savings on the weekly one hour flying lesson; Sunday was Gliding, but without any transport and a non-existent bus service the peninsula of Fife was just a barren collection of inaccessible villages, of which the new town Glenrothes was the most remote and Portmoak, the beautifully isolated gliding club, about as inaccessible and hard to get at as my dream of becoming a pilot.

But sometimes it doesn't matter if you have a long tedious journey ahead of you, if there is a definite aim in mind then you can remain blind to the boredom. The problem is that you can also remain blind to the people that you meet on the way.

The first train on a Sunday was at midday, that left me with ten miles to walk from the sleepy branch line station of Markinch to the renowned gliding club. I remember a couple of smartly dressed girls walking ahead of me, a brother or boyfriend dutifully carrying their formal dresses from the party or convention the night before. I was jealous of their quiet order and purpose as their heels clipped their way over the metal bridge and descended to the drowsy car-park, then into what looked like their dad's car and probably back to their parents semi' for a decent family lunch.

But that wasn't for me, so I strode out, ambitious and anxious to put the placid town that had already arrived at its destination behind me, and start on the road to my own. I had a pocket radio for company and remember pressing it to my ear and tuning into the Noel Edmonds radio show with John Geilgud, marvelling how I could gain access to such sedentary Sunday listening amidst these ominous hills and slowly passing fields of sheep. The road took me through Glenrothes, the strange new town concrete oasis of shopping complexes and well lit parking areas set amidst a no-man's-land of rolling foothills and farmland. A strange contrast, but uniformly barren on an early 1980's Sunday morning.

I knew I had a mission, banished to Scotland (see chapter 8) I wanted to be an RAF pilot more than ever and I knew that just gaining a pilot's licence might not be enough. 'And what else do you do with your spare time?' they'd ask at the interview, 'Gliding' I'd reply, thereby giving the impression that I lived for flying. In fact when I wasn't swatting for flying exams, or performing my thoroughly tedious job of setting up the Rapier missile site by lifting back-breakingly heavy green boxes of various sizes on a regular basis, I'd be reading one of Richard Bach's adventures with his biplanes, so I guess I really did live for 'it' - whatever 'it' was. I think, looking back 'it' was 'escape' - who knew whether the actual job of flying was to my taste? The idea seemed one of pure escapism, despite my idyllic surroundings being the dream of many retired folk and the odd ambitious glider pilot; to me right now it was a prison, the road of ambition was the one between Glenrothes and Portmoak, the fact it was made of blank tarmac rather than yellow brick didn't matter.

By the mid-afternoon I could see a tug-plane casually drifting into the air amidst the green mountains surrounding Loch

Leven. There was activity by the wooden hut and I felt apprehensive - I'm expecting it to be expensive and exclusive. I'd felt this way before when I'd tried to join a tennis club at fifteen; I'd cycle seven miles to Gosport, then be too shy to walk into the bar and ask for a game. What a waste of time that turned out to be; I got one game of tennis after forking out for a year's membership; and that was against a few charity minded teenagers who took pity as they watched me dedicate myself to hitting a ball against a wall pretending it was an opponent (for one brief moment I thought of Wimbledon as my future, despite having a wall as my main competitor - such was the sport of Tennis in the UK for a fifteen year old). So nervously I started down the muddy track and considered myself committed, past the assortment of parked cars - not all of which were shining BMW's - some real bangers in fact. There were people helping to pull in cables, someone driving an old battered truck, another scooping up rubble with an old grey vintage tractor, and others washing dishes at the serving hatch. No-one accosted me and asked what I wanted, in fact nothing like a business-run flying club at all. Where was the Chief Instructor with his clipboard and tie?   Where were the pretentious types with their 'wings', scarves and friendly condescension? I timidly looked around the clubhouse with its faded drawings of 'what to do in the event of' sketched by once keen basic students, drawn up while they waited for the wind to be gentle enough to let them go on their first solo; the ever present, slightly torn poster of the various cloud types that hangs on the wall for a splash of colour rather than any relevance to gliding. Still no one around, I ask the washer-upper and he tells me to have a word with the bloke on the tractor. This really wasn't what I expected, it was all so unassuming, matter of fact, without ambitious types trying to be jet pilots.

I wandered out to the man in an old, grey boiler suit sitting atop the rickety old machine. He appeared to be diligently shovelling cinders with the scoop attachment in an attempt to fill in potholes in the approach road; I was impressed that the club had enough money to employ a grounds-man. He was weather-worn and dishevelled, dressed in an old grey set of overalls I should have recognised from my days at Swinderby; he carefully climbed down from the tractor to adjust the attachment to the scoop, and it was then I approached and asked him where I should go to see someone about joining the club. He nodded, as if he got these queries all the time and distractedly told me to put my name on the list over by the launch where all the people were congregating, and I should be up in an hour or so. That simple. No membership card, no initial payment, no pre-flight briefing. He then climbed back onto the grey vintage tractor and carried on shovelling. This was all a bit off-putting, I expected at least a membership card, to be welcomed into the club, meet with fellow budding pilots and talk serious flying with top-notch gliding instructors. It was if they were purists just interested in gliding.

With my name on the list I joined the others and began to realise that everyone around me were also quite new to this. I found myself hauling in cables, driving the winch van, holding onto wing-tips, swapping the odd comment about the beautiful island of St Serfs in the middle of the loch. No glamour. In fact, it was hard graft that I didn't need, and I had that ten mile walk back to the station to think about...

Not long before late evening arrived, and a few lights were beginning to dot around Kinross on the other side of the loch making the view even more stunningly beautiful, when I was invited to climb into the empty wooden seat that comprised the cockpit of the K13 glider. The man in the boiler-suit wandered over, presumably to drive the winch vehicle; but no, he spoke to me in that same distracted but assured way; 'Yeah, just hop in the front and we'll get you sorted, you had your parachute brief?' I hadn't, and he proceeded to explain exactly what to do in the event of the wings falling off. He covered everything quietly and apparently without thinking too hard about it before - hang on - easing himself into the seat behind me. What was this? Is he going to just hop in and claim to be an instructor? He's the grounds man... did anyone realise that the grounds man was in the instructor's seat? Strangely, no-one was telling him what to do. He called across to the man on the wing-tip 'Don - we'll make this the last one, okay?' 'Righto Andy', came the reply. The cockpit checks were done and he showed only casual interest as I proudly announced that I had been taking powered flying lessons - jealousy I thought.

Soon we were creaking and sailing up into the evening air over the black loch, the wood and doped canvas contraption groaning like a graceful yacht. Suddenly we were alone, six inches from a thousand foot drop and I was trusting my life to a boiler-suited grounds-man that had just jumped in the back seat.

The villages had suddenly become clusters of yellow dots huddled against the slopes of the ridge far below. I felt precariously balanced but the ten mile walk suddenly felt worthwhile. I glanced at the variometer and it showed we were in rising air as we caught the lift from the edge of Ben Lomond. Immediately the man in the back banked hard to catch it and stay within this invisible bubble of air. 'It's all yours' he called in his same casual manner and I shakily started to try and hold the glider in a straight line, pointing down the ridge. 'Er, you're cross-controlling there, you see that slip ball out to the right?' I looked, 'Now look at the turn indicator, it's out to the left, try and balance aileron with rudder' he's right, I thought. Flying a glider needed a bit more finesse than I'd been used to. I wondered if he knew about powered flying, 'not the same as a Cessna' I called by way of an excuse. 'Yeah well, different ball game that - keep an eye on the ridge line, try and turn here and keep the bank on, stay within the lift - too much rudder again'. My excuse had fallen flat; did he really know that much about Cessnas? Could he really sympathise if he hadn't progressed beyond a mere gliding field?

It was soon time to land, and as we breezed across the darkening fields of sheep and the placid black mirror of the Loch in a shallow, arcing curve to finally level our wings and commence a landing run, all too soon we were skimming over the earth, then settling onto the damp grass with the sound of gentle scything before the full weight of the glider touching down began to turn the single wheel undercarriage, and we became a trundling, awkward mass of bouncing wings and ungainly metal struts as the glider slowed down, like a graceful yacht beaching against a sandbank. The sky yacht had become a bumpy rolling go-cart as we rolled to a standstill, then the wings hung suspended, balanced by aileron, until they slowly tilted to one side and confirmed our return to tedious real life. Silence.

The walk back to Markinch railway station was easy, all I could think of was sailing along that ridge, looking down on those yellow dots as I marched along the straight road, oblivious to the lifeless streets. I may as well have just arrived back from another planet, such was the kick, and that feeling would see me through a week of lifting heavy boxes of various sizes until the next weekend.

But It was some years later and I was still spending my weekends gliding, this time amidst the relatively less dramatic countryside of the Yorkshire Moors whilst undergoing jet training. Just as I was standing on the Dishforth tarmac awaiting my turn to take-off, the news came of my gliding instructor's death. He had been towing a glider into the air at Portmoak, apparently he hadn't stood a chance and many of the members were in tears. Why did everyone know his name? This club was hundreds of miles away from Portmoak. 'I remember that name', I said, quietly, to one of the instructors, 'I flew with him'. 'Lucky you', came the reply, I enquired why; 'that guy lived for flying', he went on to describe how this man, the man that I thought was the grounds man, was a display pilot with the Red Arrows, before that, Lightnings, 'did I know that'? He asked. No, I didn't.

Then I remembered that evening flight again, how I'd wondered whether he could fly powered aircraft, how I'd thought he was just the odd-job man, how he'd ignored my snobbery and excuses and shown me such a peaceful world along that mountain ridge...and I kept quiet.

Chapter 2

'You're not a natural pilot'

Flash forward two momentous years...

I walked into the inner sanctum of flying knowledge with my still newly-pressed flying suit and creaky new leather flying boots ready for my first welcoming handshake and 'well done you're part of the elite' that must be the back slapping accorded all trainee jet pilots who've made it through sixty ground exams, eighteen weeks of officer square-bashing and discovered quite by chance that they've got perfect vision, perfect hearing and with legs and arms roughly the same length. He had a moustache, a casually discarded, battered officer's cap and the walls were decorated like any flight commander's office in the movies - framed picture of a Vulcan, a Lightning, a Jet Provost, the odd trophy on the desk, a stack of files, a phone and an intercom. Behind all this sat my hard-boiled flight commander looking at me sternly - it was a scene from the Battle of Britain - I actually expected him to say 'look out for the Hun in the sun and stick to me like glue'...but he didn't... 'Let me start by telling you this...' wiry and relatively short, he had an aura that made you instantly listen, conveying the requisite pissed off attitude towards paper work and yet gave off an air of tired professionalism that would have him shooting down Mig 29s this Friday afternoon if called upon...I eagerly anticipated the pep talk I'd been aiming at all these years...

'You're not a natural pilot, Tallack'.

All confidence, bravado and innate flying skill suddenly evaporated... and that was it, my first career interview after fighting for years to get where I was, after A levels, IQ tests, years of Air Cadets, glider flying, powered flying and even building scale models of most the aircraft I wanted to fly - this bombshell, this denial of my ability. Should I pack up and go home now? I let it sink in. 'You're going to have to work at this' he sat, looking me straight in the eye, coveted flight lieutenant's stripes on the shoulder of his worn flying suit, a moustache I wouldn't be able to grow in a lifetime. Here it was, the entrance into a world of fantasy - and the gatekeeper surveyed me with suspicion from across the service-issue desk.

And that is the story I want to tell you, the tale of someone fighting his way to become a pilot despite the frowns and shaking of heads. Sometimes I think I have to work incredibly hard to reach a level of mediocrity many would just give up on as frankly, not being worth it, and then just as suddenly I'm on my own in a fast jet sailing between the cumulus as if I was born to this. There's many muck ups, not just my own, and it's certainly not a boy's own tale of adventure written to inspire. My time in the RAF is filled with anecdote because, perhaps, I wasn't supposed to be there - I was an outsider too busy observing rather than being too busy getting into trouble in Limmasol. But as a result you've got someone who can report events as they happened, because otherwise these stories will continue to do the rounds of bars and no one else will know them save the aircrew and perhaps their families. So settle in, do up your harness, check your ejector seat pins are stowed, all clear? Start her up. But let me warn you...

This is not Bravo Two-Zero. Nothing about the SAS or how I defeated the Iraqis single-handed, although all these people do make an appearance. No, this short book is a collection of short flying stories; some funny, some serious, some with an important learning curve for me; but hopefully most importantly of all - entertaining for you.   I make no claims of heroism short of actively having the guts to turn away from what I really wanted to do towards the end. A heroism of inaction based on conscience - if you like.

I don't know what I expected by aiming to join the RAF as a Pilot - escape from a small town? A sense of Challenge - like an Arthurian Knight on a quest? The freedom of the skies? An eventual job in the Airlines? Decent material to start writing a book with?   Let's face it, I didn't even know whether I liked flying, I looked up to the sky saw a jet and thought - that's what I want to do. It wasn't quite that simple but not far off.

For an eleven year old who got in too many arguments and fights (usually losing the fight after having won the argument) it was surprising to find a sudden sense of indignation and confidence when faced with a short documentary about Russian aircraft being escorted out of British airspace by Phantom jets. We were being threatened! Brought up on Commando books and Gus' Gorillas I was still in a post Second World War mood and it seemed all that was British was being threatened; I had to do something and quick. Air Cadets, A levels, application forms...

Did I really think I could make it? Or did I just feel that I should at least have a half-hearted try?   By eighteen I was armed with nothing more than a couple of 'A' levels and a good set of apprentice served mates who had no interest or intention to do such things - which turned out to be a blessing in later months.

So I'm going to tell you via a series of forty-odd short stories how I went from twenty year old naïve youth, hell bent on passionate bravura and a need to prove myself, to exactly the same idiot with thirty two years added on.   I saw some things, I felt some emotion, I lost acquaintances and fired lots of weapons, I began to see the enemy as something else and I want to tell you about that journey, with hopefully some laughs on the way.   I also hope this might go some way to explaining why I have no need to play the 'Alpha male' and force my hand all the time, much to the mystification of those around me these days; I don't think it gets you very far.

I dedicate this to all my old friends who I worked with in the RAF. You may have thought I was a non-drinking fitness fanatic who really didn't fit in, and you were right, but I'd trust my life to the lot of you.

Chapter 3

Single to Swinderby

You see, your problem is that you lack self-confidence…'

The driving instructor was known for his confrontational 'tell it like it is' stance and barked his observations like a bullying older brother. I didn't know where to find this thing called 'self-confidence'. No one does. So remember that all you wannabe Pilots, you'll hear a lot of that rubbish about qualities you can't have until you've got a bit of experience under your belt. It's not about confidence, it's about experience - something most people can get, so go out there and get it. You get some hard earned experience under your belt, you'll find you have confidence.

My two schoolmates from the state school sixth form had both got in - one as an RAF Regiment Officer, the other as a Pilot, and I was left behind - no instant career at the end of 'A' levels and faced with joining as a squaddie - an airman. A few weeks previous I'd received the infamous thin piece of paper in the post saying I'd failed Pilot selection and I'd failed Royal Marine Officer Selection.   Eighteen, and life surrounded in me in bits.

I remember sitting in the small back room in the RAF careers office on my own in Portsmouth; the rotund and homely Sergeant had set the paper in front of me, supplied an HB pencil and I was to attempt the simple questions to confirm I wasn't too stupid to join the 'RAF Regiment' – in other words the RAF's army, the 'Rockapes' – laughed at by the rest of the RAF for being commonly thought of as 'thick' – but so what – they were the guard force, the bruisers, the soldiers who did the fighting. I'd failed Pilot selection and was at the end of my A levels with my options and dreams disappearing in smoke. My Mum was telling me to get a job and my Dad was already despairing about me; it seemed that life was over, I'd been written off and I wasn't yet out of my teens.

I made sure every question was answered carefully. The Sergeant poked his head round the corner to see whether I'd finished. I hadn't. My confrontational driving instructor often mentioned a student friend of mine he also taught and who was so much more confident, more 'leadership material' – he'd got in as a Navigator – so there it was, proof that I was a lesser human being. And now here I was, taking the squaddie test for the RAF to end up a sweeper-upper in some hangar.

'We've checked your scores'.

The RAF Sergeant stood over me with a slightly embarrassed air.

'And they're just acceptable – you took the maximum amount of time you know'.

I replied that I wanted to be as accurate as possible, feeling like the thickest shit on the planet, that my driving instructor had clearly been right. I wasn't fit to do anything, what a stupid, embarrassing ambition.

'And we can't take you for a year – they're full up'.

So I got a job on a pig farm and discovered hard graft, before arguing with the owner about how he could feed his pigs more efficiently, and was sacked the next day – I like to think because of my ideas being a challenge to his pride, but inwardly knowing it was because I was pretty bloody slow at mucking out all nine of the pig pens and nearly turning the tractor over (didn't seem to matter that I'd never driven a car before). As I collected my wages from the nervous farmer's wife, she gave me an apologetic smile and I felt like the most incompetent eighteen year old on the planet.

So one week I was in the dole queue, the next week I was on the other side of the counter as a clerk dishing out the cheques. This was not the autobiographical route I had expected to take, it didn't fit the picture; my mates from school who hadn't joined the forces all worked as apprentices in local firms and had cash for nightclubs, Chinese takeaways and pizza; my old schoolmate Maz would lend me the money for the Sunday night takeaway. It was a happy existence but my sights were still set on the RAF and it meant escape, excitement even that ambiguous word 'patriotism' - which seemed completely fine back then.

I don't know when I turned, but I decided that this driving instructor needed ditching. How could I be that bad when he never let me reverse round corners? He slammed the phone down on me and practically threw the cash he owed me out of the window in his passing car. But I had cautiously made a stand, booked in with BSM and passed immediately. That was a clue. Perhaps I should begin to ignore the idiots who say things outside their imagination can't be done.

After a year I had saved £650 and bought a car. Late September - I went to discos, had a brilliant group of disco-going mates, a regular club where we'd go and drink, a job and met someone I'd fallen in love with – I was always doing that – but this time the girl actually seemed interested. All good for the confidence, which is when the RAF called to remind me I'd made a date with them...

I always remember the office – this time in Southampton and underground like a secret bunker; the curtain was drawn back and there on the wall was the special speech we had to read out whilst holding the bible. It all seemed a bit over the top. I read out the words and promised my allegiance to Queen and Country, thinking that was pretty obvious since I was trying to sign up for nine years. It was then that they issued me the ticket.

It said 'single' to Newark.

I looked at the pink ticket at the railway station. It had begun to feel like a prison sentence. 'Single'. Not 'return', I was never coming back.

On the platform at Fareham railway station, my girlfriend and I said the things that teenagers say to each other about 'always' and genuinely not wanting to part, not realising that within a two years we'd split amid bitter jealousies and the strain of living four hundred miles away. For now she waved me off from the platform and I really missed her. I missed the life I'd grown to love... I was supposed to be happy, here was everything; out there, through the approaching railway tunnel there was merely possibility. I went with possibility.

About a hundred of us walked into the unfashionable and dejected echoing hall in RAF Swinderby with downturned 'D' shaped windows and looked for my name – there it was written on a loose piece of card and placed on a wooden chair with my service number and heavy canvas holdall. I was to sit on the chair. People began to shout at us. I was to do as I was told. I missed her. I missed Fareham, when could I go and see my mates?

'Remember the number' barked the Corporal, and I still do to this day, especially when some twat was interrogating me in the mountains of North Wales. But that's later.

I wasn't sure, but perhaps self-confidence was going to appear somewhere... it didn't feel like it was going to be anytime soon.

The six weeks at Swinderby quickly became an exercise in homesickness. We shared dormitories of about sixteen iron beds lined up with a wooden locker at the side on a polished lino floor which would gather dust by just looking at it, a loudspeaker hung on the wall at the head of the room like a scene from 1984 and we nodded and put our things away nervously, awaiting the start. We'd bought into a fascist dictatorship, voluntarily.

I don't remember when it started, but suddenly we were being shouted at and told everything had to be clean for tomorrow morning, we were to wear not uniforms but ridiculous overalls with a belt round the middle that made us look like 'Odd Job' from 'Carry On Screaming'. We looked like a bunch of internees at a mental asylum; I would say 'Correction Unit' but we clearly didn't look capable of carrying out a robbery, let alone fighting a war. We soon learned that the Corporal that shouted continually was a man capable of deciding whether we returned to our girlfriends and parents or not - and we frequently didn't. His threats were frequently carried out, and we submitted to the threats by doing everything we were told, it was only later at Catterick that the bullying really started.

I remember walking into the NAAFI bar during a rare night off (as long as the room is spotless by tomorrow by 7am), surrounded by losers like me still dressed in overalls and belts - most seemed to be enjoying themselves as a very bad stripper went through her paces and Human League (Don't You Want Me) played in the TV room on Top Of The Pops. I thought the story in the video was me and my girlfriend - she wasn't a waitress in a cocktail bar but she DID work as a hairdresser and I was going to lose her; and all I would have would be the likes of the ugly stripper in the room next door being cheered on by the teenagers who'd just discovered alcohol. This was it, my life was mapped out, I should have stayed in Fareham.

We were being trained for all trades in the RAF, so there were cooks, drivers, technicians, all together being hammered by inspections and marching up and down before specialising in our trades. Of course the 'Rockapes' as the few of us were known, were considered the brainless ones who just shot people and did assault courses. We had a lot more of this to come and I was beginning to think my choices had been ill-informed; but then I looked up to the clear blue sky in the early morning parade and, whilst the Corporal shouted at us in the usual monotone, I imagined jumping out of a plane into that purity of blueness and leading the life of a paratrooper in the elite 2 Squadron; that would be my inspiration, my carrot to get me through the next sixteen weeks, but that all seemed about thirty years away. If I was going into the Regiment I was definitely going to be a part of the elite para' unit, I had a lot to prove, and I have to confess my aim of being a pilot was being closely followed and at times eclipsed by the physical challenge of getting into the para' unit of II squadron and then applying for the SAS.

But right now that was a long way away. At least twenty six weeks...

We marched past blocks where the bedding was being thrown out of the windows if a room had failed an inspection, we marched up and down in a hangar where the Corporal got more and more angry with all fifty of us and made us stay in to do more marching on Saturday and Sunday. You think you've got a weekend, then you find yourself staring at the rivets on the wall of the hanger for several hours. Pointless, our lives were cleaning, cleaning, marching, cleaning.   We did it because we all wanted to get over this hurdle, we all thought there was a secret awaiting us that wasn't obvious right now - this was the gateway and they didn't want to let us in.   Can you make the grade? That was how the advert went, and we wanted to make the grade, even if it appeared the 'grade' was wearing dumb overalls and marching up and down. Later I would watch amazing things being done with this mass co-operation; but was it achieved here at Swinderby? By fear of authority? Did we need to be broken down like this first?

Cut to the shower room - I'm laying on the floor asleep at 1:30am being woken by a Corporal with a toothbrush in my hand being made to clean the tiles, the others are desperately polishing the floor of the dormitory after a Regiment Corporal had poured a mass of polish into the middle and said we'd better start rubbing it in or it'll go solid in minutes - after we'd spent an hour shining that very floor - but that was Catterick - and yet to come.

In the midst of these days the characters developed; my good friend Mark was from Portsmouth, we both ran in the evenings by sneaking out of the camp in running kit and getting in a quick half hour session. We talked of our hopes with 2 squadron, of what to expect, where this was going. He was quite a 'lad' given to quick reactions and a real dedication to training, so at least here was someone I could get on with.

Every week my girlfriend would write to me and keep me sane; perfumed letters covered in all the right acronyms of 'SWALK' and the like. It was a constant reminder of what I was missing and her photo sat in my locker and was my constant course of hope and aspiration. I look back and think perhaps this wasn't the best thing, to have this pull to get back home was affecting me in a negative way, but I decided that if I failed I would also lose her, and that I had to pass in order to keep her and provide a future for us both. I considered the dole office I'd been working in as I swept, shined, polished and scrubbed with Brasso, wax, detergent, listening to George Benson on the newly acquired 'Walkman' - and with that a revolution in cleaning - sweeping up to Michael Jackson on the headphones 'Working Day and Night' made the evenings bearable. But thoughts of the pig farm, any work in Fareham, now was the time to leave and enjoy the eighties for all it offered... but I stuck it. Here was the choice, the sacrifice, the eventual loss; but here was also the empty, cold, church hall rehearsal room before the actors arrive and the performance begins. You needed vision, the same vision that made me take that driving test after being told I was useless and lacked confidence.

The hole that was 'Swindits' soon became a memory as we marched past on a freezing, snow covered morning with my parents and girlfriend in attendance. Catterick was next - sixteen weeks learning to be an RAF Regiment Gunner, and I wasn't looking forward to it. More marching, more cleaning,

21

more shouting, very little soldiering. When was I going to start jumping out of aircraft?

Chapter 4

Stubborn confidence – gets me nowhere

'Now remove the barrel.'

It wouldn't budge.

'It's jammed Corporal'.

'Really?'

Oh dear, the Regiment Corporal didn't believe me - he'd used that tone of voice. But I heroically stayed with it.

'Yep – that's jammed Corporal'.

It was my TOET test, I have no idea what that stands for – there was so many of them – but this was a pass or fail on the General Purpose Machine Gun at Catterick – or 'gimpy' as it's affectionately known; I had to load, unload, make safe and generally strip the whole thing down and put it back together again in front of an RAF Regiment Corporal – this one had parachute wings on his arm – which meant he'd jumped out of planes and done all the stuff I wanted to do; bearing mind Corporals had become a surrogate Victorian parent in the past six weeks; they had the power to keep you in at the weekend and make you peel potatoes every evening for however long they wanted. Girlfriends didn't understand; if they didn't like the way you made your bed or stamped your foot when coming to attention – that was your weekend being spent marching up and down.

So there I was doggedly sticking to my gun – literally. The bloody barrel wouldn't come off. I lifted the handle, turned it ninety degrees and pulled... nothing.

'Are you absolutely sure you're doing it right Airman?'

'Yes Corporal'.

Back coursed. That meant doing the last six weeks of hell all over again. I'm not sure I could face it. All because of this bloody bleeding barrel not coming off.

'Okay. So you're telling me that this gimpy is faulty? That the barrel is stuck and the gun is U/S'?

'Yes, definitely Corporal'.

'Were you told to *lift* the barrel before turning it ninety degrees?'

'Yes Corporal'.

'Okay – so just for the sake of argument – try not lifting it before turning it ninety degrees'.

I was pissed off now – I'd clearly failed the whole dam test. Re-do the whole six weeks with the new intake of shaven headed idiots? Polishing the floor at 2am again. Here we go.

'That's not what I was taught Corporal (I'd decided to hang on to this pathetic argument).

'Really. Okay so – just for interest's sake – do it anyway. Don't lift the handle, just turn ninety degrees and push.

So this is what I do. The barrel slides straight off just like it was designed that way, mainly because it was. I am exposed as a lying failure that is about to shout 'fuck this' and storm out if it wasn't for the fact that I'd be physically kicked out the door by the Corporal before I even got the 'F' out.

'Look at that – it seems to work Airman.'

I say nothing. I'm fuming. My head bows as I stare at the barrel in my hands – the un-doer of so much cleaning, drill, marching, assault courses, kit pressing. My entire future has been crushed by this barrel.

'Now I want you to put that barrel back on then take it off again – without lifting it'.

We'd had one airman given a week's work in the cookhouse because his bed sheet was creased *under* the blanket, Mark was made to run back and forth up and down the range with an ammo box on his back because he laughed at the wrong time, he went AWOL the next day. Sometimes it was racism, sometimes it was thuggery, sometimes it was the fact they just didn't like you – find a weakness they'd exploit it. I awaited my fate.

'Now put that barrel back on the gun and take it off again thirty times – count as you do it'.

I resign my self to my fate and allow the humiliation to continue. One, two, three –

The Corporal interrupts as I reach twenty eight.

'On the last go I want you to tell me exactly what you think of me Airman'.

I slot the barrel back onto the bastard gimpy one last time. Take a deep breath, realise I've got away with it. Glad no-one else can hear me.

'Corporal _____ knows exactly what he's talking about'.

'Fuck off' is his order.

I scurry out, never forgetting how to take that barrel off the gimpy. Thankful to find a moment of humanity in this sixteen weeks of hell.

Chapter 5
Hand-picked volunteers

So here we were, at the end of sixteen weeks with shaven heads, marching up and down the parade square in fear of being 'volunteered' and sent to 'QCS' - The Queen's Colour Squadron'. Some us wore glasses even though we didn't normally, I was about to be charged for bending my arms and getting out of step, we were just on the edge of being stamped as only a few wanted to be picked for this unit.

It was the RAF's guards unit - used for ceremonial duties like guarding Buckingham Palace and marching in clever formations at the Royal Tournament. Actually now I think of it, it might have been quite good fun - based outside London and getting to perform clever rifle drill - what the hell. But to me at twenty, this was toy soldier crap and had to be avoided. Yet here we were - actively being chosen by the barking mad Colour Sergeant with the goggle eyes, the chains in his trousers (to keep them straight), the pace stick and the boots that clicked on the gritless tarmac (the grit had been swept up by numerous intakes), he was a Warrant Officer and a product of the QCS – The Queen's Colour Squadron (the formation drill team) we really didn't want to become him. I look back on him as man having a laugh - mid forties - wife and kids - several years of this and you just want to shock and scare the recruits so that they'll shut up and get on with it.   Probably more satisfying than teaching.

Needless to say it was all unnecessary; it was well known that I and a few others were hell-bent on getting into the elite 2 squadron parachute unit and we were terrified we'd not be allowed to go if we were volunteered for the dreaded QCS. So I bent my arms, got out of step, one wore glasses and I was threatened with a charge. Turns out our application for the elite parachuting II Squadron prevented us being selected for QCS. Hurrah. Here comes the parachuting, running, leaping out of planes stuff. I guess I didn't really know myself that well...

I was posted to Hullavington - the home of 2 squadron - to become an 'Airborne Warrior'; to jump out of planes and run great distances with rucksacks, to eventually apply for the SAS maybe. I was excited. I arrived at Chippenham station with everything I owned crammed into seven bags still wearing my RAF number one uniform (it was regulation we travel in uniform); I put the bulging canvas tube sack over my neck, two bags around my neck and carried the four holdalls in both hands. Poor old Mark had been kicked out for going AWOL, but blonde, shaven-headed US Marine styled Greg had become another fellow mate in this lofty aim of becoming a paratrooper. It was the 1st April 1982.

I picked up The Sun in the railway carriage as we bumped along towards Chippenham, wondering how we'd cover the five miles from the station to the camp; the headlines read that a small group of islands called the Falklands had been invaded. Argentina? This wasn't quite right; first of all I hadn't finished training so the timing was all wrong; secondly Russia was the threat, not some country in South America. Hopefully I'd get the parachute training in first and not miss out. Little did I realise that the next hundred days would see 255 British and 649 Argentinian dead, and my career a smouldering wreck.

Chapter 6

'Gimpy's my weapon...'

'X' was a bit arrogant, already a reservist parachutist so he'd done all this before and was pretty fit – he didn't bother with training in the evening, unlike the rest of us. He was also black - and I'd never known racism could be so blatant.

He got a lot of shit, especially from the Sergeant and the Corporal who in one instance ripped the sheets off his bed, pointed to the minute crease underneath the blankets, said 'look you B...B... that's a crease, two weeks in the cookhouse'. And that's what he got, two weeks extra duties in the evening because, well, they didn't like him. To say we raw recruits weren't surprised is an understatement; we'd already lost Mark AWOL after they'd bullied him into running several times up and down the rifle range with an ammo box - that didn't worry him, but the name calling of 'half cast' did. A couple of our training NCOs were nasty, vindictive types and were eventually demoted for bullying. When you see military training in war films you don't see the bit where they actually want you to fail, these really did.

But 'X' kept on, ignoring the insults, head down, did what he had to do, nothing more. When it came to our weapon training exams he turned up with the usual shrug of his shoulders – and promptly failed the basic rifle exam. He walked out with the timeless remark we all chorused and taunted him with:

'Gimpy's my weapon'.

The General Purpose Machine Gun, or GPMG for short, is nicknamed the 'Gimpy'. His excuse was that he was already a specialist on this weapon, not the rifle, and that was why he had failed. We shook our heads, and whenever anyone messed up, be it losing at darts, coming second on the assault course, the excuse that would echo around was 'ah well, Gimpy's my weapon'.

'X' said nothing. Took it in his stride. Arrogant to the end.

We all had abuse - my nickname was either 'Badger' or 'Some bird shit on my Head' (I had a grey patch in my hair) and the second seemed to stick amongst the Corporals; we had 'Taff' for the Welsh, 'Jock' for the Scots, 'Minger' for anyone who didn't wash, in fact anything that was abusive and separated you from the rest, especially if you didn't like it, became your nickname. By no means is this trying to explain the racist name calling as appropriate or understandable, but it explains how this stuff develops. Nevertheless, 'X' just kept on.

Eventually we were posted to our units; myself, 'X' and another went to the infamous II Squadron, the elite parachute unit, we were all volunteers and turned up at Hullavington to begin the pre-pre-para, but we hadn't yet got our wings so would act as near enough servants to the established old hands on the Squadron; naturally we commanded very little respect and were actively threatened with initiation at any moment, whatever that was. We tentatively grabbed our bed-spaces amongst the established soldiers in the block and this was terrifying in itself as I had a bed opposite two Zulu shields with crossed spears and a giant stereo system; turns out the squadron was at least 50%

African-Caribbean, the rest were from Liverpool and Scotland's rough estates; I'd just love to have seen our Corporals posted here - but it was also the fittest, funniest and proudest group of soldiers I'd ever had the honour to spend time with. Only two were removed for psychopathic tendencies.

But 'X' was still being chided... this time there was no racial aspect, he was being refreshingly singled out just for lack of training in the evening. So he started training with us and began to play the game. But soon he would have the last laugh.

We took part in an exercise on Salisbury Plain playing a four-man enemy hidden in a woods to the rest of the Squadron; we buried 'X' with his machine gun, well camouflaged, whilst the rest of us were overrun by the Squad whilst we fired pencil flares at them. Not a good idea... the para' unit leapt out of their armoured personnel carriers and skirmished towards us like a pack of hungry hyenas; we were firing live flares and they had blanks – but we were definitely more scared than the hooligans coming at us – naturally we were roughed up for causing them this disturbance, then trussed up and chucked in the back of troop transporters; but one of us were missing - the squad searched the woods - they knew there was one more, but couldn't find him. Finally, they gathered together in a clearing before conducting a formal man-hunt, 'ratattat' goes the machine gun as 'X' opens up with the 'Gimpy' from about five feet away, buried underneath the bush they're practically standing on. The clearly decimated squad reacts with 'hang on - that's not right'. X has just wiped out the entire bunch in one go. Stunned silence. Gimpy was indeed his weapon.

I, as I was to find out later, was very fit, but bloody useless emotionally. Best I stick to writing.

I saw 'X' in Chippenham several years later. Confident as ever, Para wings, a complete success at what he had set out to achieve. He'd kept his head down, suffered abuse in a time when people got away with it. Arrogant? Perhaps. Perhaps that is what got him through.

Good on him. I think he had the long view.

Chapter 7

The ten miler

Ten miles. Running. With a rifle and kit. I remember the shuffle of our feet, the nestling of the rifle on my right ammo pouch, the way I'd customised my kit so that none of the mess tins rattled on my back, it weighed about twenty five pounds, the rifle nine, It was fitted to my body with the same precision given a Tour de France cyclist pays to his bike; It was a ten mile race with thirty-five pounds of kit, the last test of the past six weeks of pre-para selection tests and I was going to try and win it.

The eight of us had been to Scotland racing up mountains with our boss on a walky-talky checking up with the squadron about the Falklands and whether we were needed. Each night the lorries dropped us off and we raced back to camp, me to eat a pound of Milky bar and Greg to eat his nightly intake of Caingorm fish and chips. Now here we were, the last week of six spent getting faster and faster round the assault course, swim tests, long distance races, now we were up on the Scottish mountains with a dogged geordie physical training instructor ('right chasps') happily suggesting, after a day climbing mountains, that we finish the day with a six-ten mile race home.

Greg stood out as a top walker with plenty of stamina - the blonde, blue eyed hero would have beaten me on the walking tasks but I could usually outrun him. I was carrying all sorts of 'essentials' for a ten mile race; an overnight bivvy shelter, a full water bottle, ammo pouches, shoe cleaning kit, first aid kit, rifle cleaning kit, wash kit, all covered in hessian dust from the sound proofing fabric I'd wrapped it all in, all of it required kit to be carried on this final test of pre-para selection. Don't forget the rifle - no strap allowed - but you very quickly find its centre of gravity.

I'd been training for this long before I joined the RAF; seven mile runs in the evenings – two laps of my neighbourhood dual carriageway carrying that old green rucksack with several copies of books in the back for added weight. I knew the steady sound of boot on concrete syncopated with my regular, closely monitored breathing. But here I was up against the other hopefuls, fifteen or twenty other recruits hoping to make it through the next few hours by stumbling along with this mass of green hanging off us. It was an exercise in logic as you threw one foot in front of the other and struggled against the reasoning that shouted in your ears 'why am I carrying all this stupid kit?' And you had to answer it, had to make sense of it immediately or you'd just drift to a halt within seconds, stop the rubbing pain of a blister in your boot, the rawness on your shoulders or the back pain from the scabby blisters on your back that hadn't healed from last week's charging up mountains in Scotland. You had to make sense of it all very quickly, and sort out your breathing, your jogging, the rifle slipping off that ammo pouch, trudging, breathing, clank (mess tins – bugger), slight incline, ignore the back pain, trudge on.

Pretty soon I'd separated from the bulk of the pack as we'd already established it was a race and it was down to me and two others. One was a young officer, the other was Greg - who could hump kit vast distances at great speed. All our kit was wrapped around our bodies like a well fitted glove, our rifles lodged and our t-shirts dark with sweat, we passed no words as we emerged from the back roads of Catterick and followed the dual carriageway to camp.

I was euphoric; here I was, being paid to do what I had been training to do every evening as a sixth form college kid, this time with a semi-automatic rifle, a helmet, 24 hours supply of rations in my pouches whilst families in Cortinas sped by on the A1 wondering what the hell we were playing at. Strange beings with weapons and sweat and hardship in stark contrast to the mundane trappings of happy families. For once I was in the right place. I was twenty.

'We've still got a while to go – best we pace it'.

The young officer wanted to give me some advice. All credit to him, he stayed with me and we kept each other company as we passed eight miles, he had a different style of running, arms out, a little awkward, his intelligent approach was a word of warning as I just kept listening to my innards – my stomach, my knees, my lungs, my throat, my back (ouch) my breathing, and adjusting the pace, maybe faster, maybe slower. Breathing. My black, well worn, 'racing boots' were like trainers on my feet, I'd run in this clothing so much it would be a surprise to actually run in PT kit. I loved the fact that we were on open road and this was 'work' time, not my evening run. The cars flashed past; it was like running into the Olympic stadium as the commuters on the A1 watched myself and the young officer leading the field.

Nine miles...

'Shall we come in together?' He uttered between breaths; I fancied he suggested rather than asked and it was getting to that point when the finish would soon be in sight.

The chance for glory was being snatched away.

'let's see how we feel' I lied, fully knowing that I was going to race this one to the bitter end. I think he knew it too.

Clomp, clomp, clomp, but no rattle, no rustle of kit, no banging of helmet, we had our 25 pounds tightly trussed on our backs, custom fitted from miles and miles of carrying and running with it.

Our boots were sometimes in unison, sometimes not, but were we getting faster? Were we racing? We were neck and neck, pretending to be keeping each other company, the rest were long behind, our rifles still wedged into our sides, our bivvy packs still strapped to our backs, our mess tins still quietly clanking; a muffled, rhythmic shuffle would accompany the two of us as we passed along the edge of the dual carriageway and into the airfield perimeter track of RAF Catterick. Just the airfield to go.

Now I was alive. The stadium excitement of the A1 gave way to the athletic track-feel of the airfield peri-track. This was what I lived for, this was what I trained for, this was what I was on the planet for! Somehow it felt right. Looking back, it also feels that the ability to do such feats meant that nothing could come close again, this is a peculiarly singular skill I have here, the ability to hump awkward kit very quickly between two points...

And so, gradually, ruthlessly, I opened up the pace; my accompanying collection of rifle cleaning kit and mess tins worked in unison as if every human was born with these things attached and my rifle, this nine pound killing machine, was as much a part of my life as a sweat band or a nice warm woolly hat on my head. The young officer fell away. I felt like one of the flying Finns - Vaatenan coming round the final bend.

Gone were the vindictive Sergeants and Corporals of basic training; here the three Physical Training Instructors were standing with the stopwatch and clipboards urging me on as I swept towards the final bend. I knew there was a top ten board in the gym – 'a hall of fame' for the ten miler. I wanted to be on it, and it was just me round the last bend, the last hundred metres as I sprinted past the line. I slowed to a halt, turned round to cheer the young officer in, and we then had to fireman's lift each other for two hundred metres, with kit. With the adrenaline it was easy - I felt like a Kip Keno who starts doing press ups after 26 miles. If this is soldiering I'm your man.

I got out a plastic camera and photographed the rest as they came in. 'Well done, for winning', said the chief, 'you can double time the squad back to the mess hall.' I waited for them to do their fireman's carries, then they formed up, exhausted. I'd had a rest.

'Double – time!' I shouted and I started to jog.

'Left, left, left-right left!'

'Fuck off' – came the reply from one of the squad.

He was right, it might feel alright to me but to the others it had been pretty hellish. We all had our weaknesses and for some of these wannabe paras' they'd fought through the one thing they were dreading. But the one thing we all agreed on - the next stop - was the easy bit - the jump.

It was the end of May '82 and I had passed pre-para with flying colours. I thought back to that day on the parade square at Swinderby in those ridiculous grey overalls just six months ago, when I looked up to the clear sky and thought maybe one day I'd be leaping out into that clear azure blue of freedom and sticking the finger up to all those that thought I was the nervous one, the timid one, the one who lacked self-confidence...

Apparently I was third in the top ten all time hall of fame for the final ten mile kit run. I was in front of recruits from five, ten years ago who'd gone on to the SAS. But I soon discovered, very quickly, that it wasn't all about running...

Chapter 8

'A man's gotta know his limitations…' Number 1 PTS: Parachute School

I sometimes think, without any form of intended self-pity, that I am always that last customer wandering up to the till when you've just about had enough for today. I always turn up; faceless, vacant, without any point other than to annoy and get in the way between you and knocking off for the day. I'm there when you'd really rather be anywhere else than school, that tie, that nose, blending in as always and representing faceless authority; or the anonymous hotel guest who makes your job verge on the tedious as I pitch up, expecting nothing but the usual face of indifference. Perhaps it's a sign of age, perhaps I have an in-built ability to annoy. I certainly managed it at school, my face just kept getting in the way.

But sometimes I decide that it's time to jut out, to moan about a bill, to make a stand, to damn well not blend in any more. To dare, take a leap, do those things the Hollywood stars tell you to do with the idealistic backing music - it worked for them… so yes - I was going make up for those times. This is one such story where I decided to make my mark - from here on I could walk into discos and ask women to dance, look the world in the eye, set my jaw with a sense of character; and man, did I pay the price.

'By the left, double time!' One of those situations you cannot believe happening, was happening. I barked the order and, as if by magic, my squad started running in step through the camp; but this wasn't just any ordinary squad of soldiers, this was a mixture of Marines, Paras, RAF Regiment and SAS that I was, momentarily, in command of – you believe it? Mainly because I was the only one who knew the way to the flight-line where the Tri-Star was arriving back from Port Stanley where the Falklands war heroes were about to arrive. I brought the band of elite killing machines to a halt, got them to fall out and led them around to our viewing area where we watched from a few feet as the heroes we'd been watching on the TV disembarked down the gang plank, all smiles, job done, waved at the 'maroon machines' amongst us and trundled off into the departure lounge and the rest of their lives, with war stories of Goose Green at the ready. We paid our respects, then returned to the hangar...

'Don't lose any sleep over it' said the stone faced PJI (Parachute Jump Instructor) in his light blue jump suit, 'it's one hell of a drop – a hell of a drop – but 'y'know...'

'Fuck', we all thought, some us of us actually said it, muttered, whispered. I didn't say anything. The nervous one showed weakness – he won't manage it – I thought to myself. The PJI made a throw-away comment that suggested disillusionment;

'Look I've spent the last five years teaching the SAS free fall so this is a bit of a come down for me.'

Then he ordered us to form a circle and spread the parachute between us, on a count of three we all lifted it up in the air, the pulled it down; the canopy inflated like a balloon – made of microfilm gossamer – and it was then a horror ran through me. This? This sheet of microfiche? This - is a parachute that will support a human? The balloon slowly reached the ground and disappeared into a wafer thin sheet on the floor. Strange, my hands were sweating. We then leapt out of the dummy fuselage thirty feet up and practiced our landing falls. Even then some were nervous, but not me; I was the one who'd already jumped out of a plane back when I was nineteen - this was going to be the easy bit...

Flashback to Netheravon parachute centre - 'Go!' shouts the Army Sergeant. I'm nineteen. I look down on pleasant green fields and little houses with the odd miniature road impossibly small and a giant space of air in between. What the hell was I thinking? I froze in the door. Clattering engines. Next thing I'm tumbling, I smell fresh nylon or silk, I hear fast moving fabric, I feel chords tumbling and unwinding off my back, things happen dream-like - I try to check canopy but can't look up, forgot to count - too much going on. Must be time. Can't see the parachute. In a dream I go for the reserve handle. Calm. No reason to be scared because the plane's long gone and you're on your own. I hear a crack. I look up. Beautiful... no, I mean *beautiful*, white, dark blue and red gossamer parachute blossomed in a sky so honestly blue you could kiss it. My lines were tangled. Who cares? Silence. Birds. I kick my way out of the twists. I don't know how I got here (I later think someone must have pushed me – thanks Sergeant – the report said 'saw no effort' – I cherished it). But I am here. I shout very loudly and see my mate half a mile away drifting down onto the land of ambition, dreams, my future playground; the Celtic, Pagan wonderland of Salisbury Plain. I have never felt so alive.

Back to the hangar at No1 PTS - why are my hands sweating? That was two whole years ago. The first balloon jump is on Monday and I'm still thinking about what the PJI said. So this balloon jump is different to a plane? One of my squad mentions his skydiving mate had done over 200 jumps – but only one balloon jump – and that was enough. Wet hands...

We carry on leaping out of the dummy Hercules fuselage thirty feet up and go to the bowling alley in the evening, noting how the teams always 'high five' whenever they throw a ball down the aisle and knock over a few pins. Why couldn't I just settle for ten pin bowling? We mock them but I'm secretly envious of these RAF 'techies' , admin' staff and all sorts who just seem content to go bowling; no jumping out of balloons for them. My hands still sweat – the palms? It's Thursday evening. Jump is on Monday morning. Things'll get better.

Friday is the cage brief; it's an iron crate that takes five blokes – four sad squaddies and one excessively confident PJI. I wanted to invade the PJI's mind; how was he so confident? It was rumoured some of these nutters would do a somersault out of the cage, one rode a bike out; they've also got a sick sense of humour; one squaddie changed his mind mid leap and was hanging on by his finger tips; 'here laddie' said the PJI, 'just grab my hand and I'll haul you back in'. The squaddie reached up...the PJI let out a laugh worthy of Sid James and he fell in horror. His first balloon jump. My bloody hands are still sweating dammit. I sit in the NAAFI TV room watching the Canberra come home from the Falklands; crowds cheering, flags waving, military heroes being hugged and applauded whilst I sit in this anonymous row of armchairs with a few flight line mechanics, their crisps and bottles of coke. Me, just sweating.

In the NAAFI shop I see a JVC stereo 'ghetto blaster' in silver and blue. I promise myself I'll buy it after successfully completing the course.

Meanwhile the collection of Marines, Paras and SAS shared the bunk bedded dormitory, went for runs, scrubbed boots, the RAF Regiment fellow squaddies nervously confided to each other about the thirty foot jump out the dummy fuselage being scary – so how would the 800 foot jump feel?

Firstly, I rely on authority telling me everything will be okay - even if it isn't. If someone in HM forces tells me it's okay I'll trust them. Just don't tell me the opposite, but they had. Secondly; the skydiver who'd done one balloon jump and that had been enough...why? Thirdly; there was no slipstream with a balloon jump, you just fell 200 feet in order to open the parachute. I saw myself suspended in mid air like Wily Coyote as he runs off the cliff top, his feet spinning in the air before plummeting with the sound of a rifle shot straight down. It was that bit I was having difficulty imagining.

No imagination then. That's a good thing. Just let it happen. Still my hands sweat.

Saturday morning. A whole weekend yawned before me but it felt like I had to climb a four hundred foot wall. I decided to use the tried and tested technique used by teenagers to pull women for many a year – drink - combined with my own recreational drug of excessive exercise. I walked five miles from Brize Norton into the local town and bought four cans of Blackthorn

Cider; it was my refuge in a disco and it would surely get me through the weekend in a fog of carefree blurred vision.

Didn't work. The stark walk home made me realise that I was asking far too much of the cider - even if it was four cans. The fear wouldn't go away, I played the jump over and over in my mind; the bar of the cage would be swung back, would I be first? Yeah, why not? Bravely stepping up to the mark I'd leap out into - what? Empty, vacant, nothing. Falling. Like your worst nightmare. But the wait as the balloon ascends - so high yet not high enough to open the reserve parachute in time. Sod it, forget it, another swig of the Cider. Hands still sweating, the empty road to Brize Norton arrived all too soon back at the gates. I wasn't scared of dying, that wasn't the point, I was terrified of falling; there was a wall in front of me - a psychological, unclimbable wall I kept running at but it wouldn't let me get over it. I was tired, not drunk at all, wishing I was ill. I laid in my bunk, watched TV, tried to eat, everyone was away seeing their girlfriends. I may even have rang my parents, expressing a sense of awkwardness, but they were used to it, not harsh, just expecting this to be nerves.

Night time was no escape. The awfulness of not jumping pretty well balanced out my fear of jumping. I remember the II Squadron veteran's casual but menacing remark as we waved our goodbyes for the para' course - we were off to get our beloved parachute wings:

'Don't come back without them' he murmured.

We laughed and shrugged it off. To not jump would dishonour the whole Squadron, remember that, it wasn't even a vague option. You cannot 'not' do it. It's a trifling matter of just one metre you have to move. The easy bit. The 'hard' bit had been the previous six weeks.

Flashback a couple of weeks: 'How do you think you did?' The chief instructor laughed at me over the desk - for the first time I was top of a course, the pre-para'; the notoriously tough and physical six weeks of pre-para. I couldn't believe it.

'I think I've done alright sir'.

Victorious and on my way - here I I was now this Saturday night. Sweating.

Sunday came and there was twenty four hours to the jump; I wished I was sick, I wished I was injured, dizzy, mad, brave enough to just tell them. Let's face it, if anyone was blindly happy about the balloon jump then they must be slightly mad, but how were they coping with it, and why the hell wasn't I?

Hullavington was to be the jump zone. 'Don't lose sleep over it' I remembered the jumpmaster's words, the official words of the RAF... 'it's a hell of a drop' - once again, official. Officially frightening. Normally the forces are logical - being under fire and potentially getting shot dead is described as 'advancing to contact'. I didn't mind as long as they wrote it like that, 'you might get shot at but it's *very* unlikely you'll die - really quite safe actually', that sort of make-believe permeated my self-assurance and meant I'd go into battle with the reassurance of military logic behind me. But this, this RAF official had said 'it's a hell of a drop'. If he'd have said being shot is actually painful and going into war not to be recommended, I'd probably have thought twice about the RAF. We love to believe what we're told.

Sunday drifted to Sunday night. Possibly the worst evening of my life so far. An evening that haunts me in dreams to this present day. The nightmare would occur about three times a week for many years after, now the dream comes at random and is strangely, totally convincing. The jump is on, 'don't let us down', how did I get here? 'Never mind, you're doing it to get over your nerves' - the hours are counting. Waking up from these nightmares is like being told your death sentence has been suspended.

But this really was that Monday morning and my life was about to change...

I'm not sure how we got to the hangar. I went out to the toilet at the back and spun around maybe a hundred times. My para smock billowed, mocking me. 'Didn't expect this did you? Eh? What you gonna do about it now huh?' I kept spinning, no one could see me because I was facing out onto the airfield. I was dizzy to the point of sickness, but I recovered, damn. I wanted to crumple, to vomit, to pass out, please, let me pass out. The hangar just stood, ruthlessly solid. The para students were forming up, we were all preparing to make a step into the unknown.

I walked up to one of the Sergeants, here was my choice of step, but it wasn't from the edge of the steel cradle at 800 feet, it was a few metres across the tarmac outside the hangars, I blurted the rather important words and explained that I didn't feel well, I hoped he'd get the message.

I was taken to a Flight Lieutenant who threw up his hands - what could he do? If I wasn't going to jump he couldn't do much about it. Other NCOs with para smocks shuffled about, embarrassed. Please make this quick, punch me in the face, kick me in the stomach, shout, I don't care, just get me out of here very, very quickly. There other men in the room in jumpsuits and berets; hard-nuts that I could probably thrash in a run with kit, so what, it counted for nothing, because this I couldn't do. I felt the raise of eyebrows, the shrug of shoulders.

'You realise you can never do this course again'.

I accepted my discharge and was sent back to Hullavington - to my Squadron. Oh dear. They put me in an MOD mini driven by a Parachute Regiment Major. Surprisingly pleasant, my coward status meant there as no rivalry between us and we avoided the giant elephant stomping all around the mini quite well, that was until he mentioned how he would stand and look over the edge of the Hercules ramp before jumping:

'That must be terrifying' I said in my new found cowardice.

'Of course it's terrifying' he responded with the first harshness of tone he'd shown.

'I'm always bloody terrified'. He looked at me momentarily as if I was brain dead.

'But I still do it'.

I was dropped off at the gates like a refugee awaiting deportation; luckily the squadron were on Northern Ireland training down on the south coast and wouldn't be back for a few days.

This was now, quite simply, a dangerous place to be. I'd let everyone down and I knew I had to somehow go into hiding. Just as I walked back to the telephone box a famed NCO of the

squadron who trained us in the notorious pre - pre para'
spotted me. Great. What the hell was I going to say?

"Heard you'd had some problems with sickness'.

'Yeah something like that' - I lied - nowadays you might think it's
very easy to say 'I completely fucked up and got scared'; but this
isn't your world. The closest thing I can say to you is for you to
imagine trying to explain wife-beating to your average father in
law. Not easy, incomprehensible, taboo, wrong, probably
causing a violent reaction. Yeah, well such is the philosophy of a
para' unit. It's what I wanted, and I had failed and let down the
name of the Squadron; I will expect to have the shit beaten out
of me until I'm posted elsewhere.

It wasn't a good couple of weeks. As a squaddie, you just do
what you're told, and I didn't want to be anywhere near when
the lads came back from Northern Ireland training; but I was left
to fester in an office awaiting jobs, taking messages and when
they turned up I made pretty sure I was somewhere else. Night
time was actually dangerous; one particular recruit was later
rumoured to have been kicked out for psychopathic tendencies
and was in the floor above - when you hear these people
coming in late on a Friday you realise you're on your own.
There was no Police, no Sergeant, the 'block' was ruled by
whoever claimed it when all were away for the weekend.
Sleeping downstairs you were not only a new recruit, but a new
recruit who had failed the jump course. I didn't sleep in my bed,
instead I was hiding in a wardrobe, counting the days.

Such beautiful summer evenings in 1982 Wiltshire should have
seen me celebrating my new-found status and sporting the
para' wings on my arm. It was a funny contrast to look out on

this late summer light glinting off the Bath-stone block houses of Hullavington and yet be so fearful and despondent. Did I now stop running? Did I give up all my aims and beliefs? Would my friends back home speak to me? Was I now a lesser human being?

I started thinking, no one back home had tried this, everyone outside this microcosm of fenced off barrack blocks had even thought of attempting any such thing. I had at least given it a go, if anything I was guilty of over-estimating my abilities: 'A man's gotta know his limitations' Clint Eastwood's words echoed in my head. Or perhaps I was guilty of having an over-active imagination; would Byron, Shelley or Ernest Hemingway have done it? They had all done 'brave' things, but so had I. Who's to say what might suddenly clip their Achilles heel? Was it ever tested? Had they ever fallen at the test? Would they have talked about it? Someone many years later made the observation that you learn more from failing at something than you do from succeeding. But clearly I wasn't cut out for this, I should give it all up and use my imagination.

Suddenly the door of the barrack room was burst open, I was caught dozing on my bed with the main light on. Greg and Tim burst in - they had been on the jump course with me and had all sorts of rumours about me being beaten up.

'On the night jump I went and shat myself' Uttered Greg with glee. He was genuinely astonished at my having left the course. Suddenly the healthy rivalry between us was dead. 'We heard you'd been attacked', 'Nope - they couldn't find me'. I rested on my elbow as Greg, the only friendly face I'd seen in two weeks, relayed the rest of the jumps and offered his concerns. His future still intact, mine in pieces. It was a curiously symbolic moment in that dormitory as he faced his future and I was suddenly looking elsewhere.

I was eventually interviewed and tested by a Psychiatrist at Wroughton hospital, she told me the 'good news' and said I was perfectly fit to do the jump course and could return to duty straightaway, a possibility which would induce another series of nightmares, such had the balloon jump become in my consciousness. She really didn't understand, luckily the squadron did, I was too bloody scared, not psychologically unwell. I wasn't going to be doing that again.

One further incident taught me something about the grass being greener; I was tasked as Ambulance driver for a paradrop on Salisbury plain, driving the top-heavy vehicle along the ruts and furrows with a medic on board. He referred to the lads I'd known as 'heroes', 'elite', 'super-fit', 'crack troops', when all we'd ever talk about amongst ourselves was our lack of purpose, our constant hanger sweeping, our lack of credibility in comparison to the Army parachute regiment...'Our'... The moment one was no longer a part of such a world one begins to hear the voices of the onlookers, and it was surprising. Nowadays, I will never let myself get so close to something that I don't keep a guarded eye or thought on how it is perceived outside of my own narrow vision of that world. It's easy to be cynical about the job I do - teaching - but I also know I don't get to hear those conversations where teachers are praised, but the moment I leave this world I can guarantee I'd be in conversations where there'd be an example of teaching that stirred the soul, and I go 'dam!'

I went for a run around the base, proving to myself that running wasn't just for military reasons but for therapeutic reasons as well; as I did so I came across the barrage balloon hanging tethered to its post on the outskirts of the airfield. I pondered its ineffectual shape and pointlessness on this still, cloudless summer evening. A slight breeze caught its tail and it slowly, very slowly rotated itself to look at me, like a caged elephant in a zoo finally acknowledging my presence. There was a little mouth shaped 'cup' under the nose - it looked like a laughing mouth. I couldn't believe it, it was as if the balloon was laughing at me. I couldn't help smiling at the metaphor; such a beautiful place, a fantastic ambition killed mercilessly by this beast of fabric filled with Helium. To quote Charlie Kaufman:

'if you don't risk failure, you're never going to do anything that's different to what you've already done.'

August came and the squadron had something like four weeks block leave before Ireland, it was like school holidays. I made a break for it and started cycling towards the station, bag on back. A car came past loaded with hardened squaddies from the base, one stuck his head out and I awaited the final parting abuse from the Squadron I'd let down; instead he just paused and gave me the thumbs up. I have no idea what this meant. I'm still not sure. I waved back.

Soon I would be called back from leave after a week, posted to Scotland and the rest of my life would begin.

Chapter 9

'They don't take their shots!'

'Who's supposed to be the enemy tonight?'

'2 Para'. I replied earnestly.

'Yeah yeah, said Corporal R – they just say that – won't turn up'.

Here I am, post parachute jump failure, the Falklands has finished and the heroes have come home and - me? I'm banished to Scotland. Leuchars to be exact - a coastal fighter base in need of mobile surface to air missile operators - and that was my new role as freshly failed paratrooper. Not only that but we were supposed to be defending the air-base against a bunch of bloody paratroopers in a midnight exercise. I ate a Garibaldi biscuit and looked out to the blackness of the cold, crisp lapping sea from my dugout. I was loyally defending this beach against the ever-present threat of sudden overnight invasion and immediate conversion to Communism by the Russians. The fact that it never happened, is, I think largely due to me giving up my Christmases to be on standby to man the surface to air missile site against assault. Or maybe not. I was pissed off, lacking motivation and a long way from my hairdressing girlfriend in eighties Southampton with all its neon, pastel shades and Michael Jackson hits belting out across the floor of Barbarellas, Top Rank and Floaters' night clubs.

The exercise meant we had to set up the mobile missile launcher – an interminable array of heavy green boxes and thick unwieldy cables all powered by a Hillman Imp engine and sit there with our helmets on shivering behind our rifles for about 48 hours. I spent a lot of time looking at St Andrews and thinking that perhaps I'd missed something because all the students my age at that University seemed to be having a lot more fun than me, attractive women sat around tables in bars with guys talking about stuff - all I'd done with my mates was head out to the disco and try and summon up the nerve to ask someone to dance ; to think you might just go to a bar and find yourself talking to an attractive girl without having to pull off a dance routine worthy of John Travolta seemed - well - bloody fantastic. But never mind, remain vigilant. University can wait. It's 2am in the morning. 48 hours of Beach. Sea. Cold. Bastard icy Wind. Another Garibaldi biscuit from the ration pack. Beach, sea, cold, wind,.. wait a while, do some press ups, check watch, 2:03am. Still cold. Plastic mug of over-sweet tea. More press ups, jump in trench, climb out. Examine the heavens, question existence and reason for being, wonder about that TS Eliot poem and perhaps this was what he was trying to communicate to me in that A level - he failed with me. Time now? 2:04. Two hours on, one hour off. Bloody stupid shift system. I just get my head down and it's time to wake up.

Suddenly rumour runs around the hissing radio that there's a parachute assault.

'What?'

A bloody parachute assault on to the airfield?

'At the two in the morning? Don't be daft, it's black out there, no sound of aircraft, no chutes, nothing.

I didn't see anything…

And that was just it – you never knew – for all the interminable procedure and boredom and waiting… someone might actually be planning something…

Nevertheless 'stand to' means everyone gets out their sleeping bag, cock their rifles, take up firing positions around the whirring and wheezing missile launcher. But it's black out there, cold, windy – icy windy. The only thing I can see across the runway is the distant lights of the Phantom hangars – cold white flickering across the black pool of a runway. My thoughts wander back to the stars and the lights of St Andrews…

It looks like the hangar lights have started to flicker.

But figures are running in between the hangars and me - that's what's making them flicker. Running. Towards me. Two hundred metres. They're carrying kit but moving fast – rifles – parasmock, tight fitting berets. Hundred metres. I get ready to call the password but I have to admit this doesn't look like the relief guard bringing the tea urn. I call my boss;

 'Corporal R, looks like someone is –'

 I wait. They haven't seen me as they approach the missile site. Hah - I know what I'll do, I'll surprise them and unleash hell from my SLR. Five highly trained Falkland veteran parachute regiment squaddies are about to die. This was going to be great.   I await the whites of their eyes as I hear the hurried swish of boot through grass – bloody hell they're belting along - they think they've got us on the hop, they think they'll surprise us. And yet here's little me in my trench like some Viet Cong tunnel rat about to annihilate. Wow, war is fun sometimes. My finger releases the safety catch and I stand, with the dull silhouette of the leader in my sights.

I open up with an unstoppable volley of 7.62mm blank ammunition from ten yards – my pitiless ambush ensuring that all five – yes all five - would die immediately. My rifle barks its orders - game over chaps...

Incredibly, they ignore me. Incredibly they keep coming, slightly angry that I've tried to shoot them.

Fuck you! Shouts the nearest blackened face in a Glasgow burr. Shit, I quickly realise this isn't really war but far worse - a Saturday Night bunch up with Glaswegian nutters - as I see the flash of a maroon beret and a set of Sergeant stripes in close up as he grabs my rifle by the barrel and shoves it into my stomach, pushing me back into my trench, winding me and making me lose my footing. ' Oi - umph!' I half shout as I stumble back into the muddy hole - he's already on his way without catching his breath - the other four run on past to Corporal Robinson and the other heroic defenders of the Rapier missile battery who are by now also firing their suddenly pointless pop guns; I hear a bit of shouting and then realise they've decided to capture the site, bashing the odd one of us over the head for even considering to dispute what they are clearly going to succeed in doing. They've just jumped out of a bloody plane let's face it.

I feel deflated.

'But I shot the lot.'

'Never mind' Says R, nursing his pride and actual bruises.
'They don't really follow rules.' I felt a bit sorry for him and me.

A few months later it was the Marines' turn.

This time it's daytime and I let loose with a General Purpose
Machine Gun after about fifty hours stuck on that bloody beach
as her majesty's Royal Marines decided to attack. Up they came
running at us throwing thunderflashes and firing rifles. I
swivelled round and let fly with the gimpy an unending
cacophony of ratatatatat. This time the buggers not only
ignored us but decided in broad daylight to tie all five of us up
with plastic tie grips. In five minutes we were all face down
with our legs touching our ears looking like prize chickens. In a
bloody row. There was Robbo' barking the usual orders and yet
he's right there with us – legs tied up round his ears.

It does shake your Universe somewhat when you have what
you consider a tight fighting unit with your Corporal in charge
and many exercises spent learning how to defend against
marine and para assault, but when it actually happens you end
up like this with your leader trussed up like a festive turkey.

'They didn't take their shots!' I strained and exclaimed angrily
from my face down position.

R looked at me – sideways out the corner of his eye because he
couldn't move his head that much.

'That's not the way it works.'

I begin to figure war doesn't really follow rules either. Whilst
waiting for someone to come along and cut us out of our tie
grips I consider that's probably why the Paras and Marines did
so well in the Falklands – the rules said it couldn't be done – 44

miles across hell with no choppers? And they said 'who gives a shit?'

I pondered the Russian Spetznaz parachuting in and also metaphorically not taking their shots and felt suddenly highly ineffective, slightly stupid and a bit wiser.

Having to do standby duty that Christmas of 1982 felt a little hollow to say the least. Hopefully the Russian Special Forces would give it a miss this year.

 What a year. I'd had my ambitions thrown back in my face, but couldn't see what else to do than go on trying to be a Pilot. I'd been sidetracked for a while with the parachuting, but I realised I had to get out of here and the way to do it was to sell my car to pay for flying lessons; I enrolled with Tayside Aviation to learn to fly in Dundee and It cost me everything - surviving on a couple of pound a week whilst just living for that one hour of flying training at the weekend. From a world of physical prowess I was beginning to exercise my mind, it was time to apply myself to navigation, meteorology and air law.   But I sometimes visit Salisbury plain, see the parachuting and remember the beautiful early mornings yomping across the wild expanse - and I miss it.

Chapter 10

Dealing with wild animals

I have two smoke grenades hanging from my straps and a loaded rifle with live ammunition resting in my shoulder as I crouch in the back of the Land rover that bumps along the jungle clearing, around me sit a team of hardened Falkland's veterans, red berets pulled down over their eyes, bandoliers of live ammunition wrapped over their shoulders, rifles and machine guns sticking out like a bristling porcupine ready to be attacked, if they could have had knives between their teeth and a jolly roger bandana round their heads we couldn't have looked more threatening. Which made it all the more surprising when a swarthy, beer gutted man stumbles out of the local 'Exocet' Café and gives us the Spanish sign for 'fuck you' – one arm cocked straight at us. I'm expecting a re-enactment of Bloody Sunday as the Paras, not exactly known for their diplomacy, do absolutely nothing, just ignore. Not a sound, not even a comment, prior briefing I guess. Wow. Then again, we're expecting worse; the Para' Major in the front seat turns and motions to my smoke grenades with a look of disgust on his face:

'Do you know how to use those?'

Like a petulant teenager who's just been told to go careful crossing the road, I try to nod knowingly, but all it comes out as is a nervous excessive nodding which suggests 'I think so' and does nothing to reassure his suspicion that he's got a couple of keen RAF regiment idiots seconded on patrol with him, and this promises to be quite a mission.

I volunteered for this. Posted for four months to Belize as part of my Squadron's commitment to protecting our old colony from Guatemala, I was bored; stuck in a Rapier missile bunker for a week, a week filling sandbags, then one week off. Hang on, that sounds brilliant nowadays... but back then it seemed somewhat 'lacking' in opportunity and I was missing out on my flying lessons. I had four months to waste in what I was told was 'the armpit of the world' and decided I needed some real 'soldiering' experience. I had no idea of the stories I would take home:

'Okay', said Operations; 'got a jungle patrol coming up with 2 Para' – anyone wanna go?'

Myself and one other volunteer pitched up to find the red berets slightly nervous. One year on from their famous Goose Green assault they were, surprisingly, zeroing their weapons and being briefed on what was likely to be a tricky little mission. It was going to be a drugs bust, I was a part of it.

'When have you had to zero your weapons before going on patrol?' muttered the early twenties private to another; I didn't get it, I wasn't nervous because I didn't know what they were talking about; stupidity is bliss. Then we had the brief, the Major stood up and made a matter of fact assessment of the job; 'turns out there's a village widely suspected of dealing, manufacturing and growing Cannabis, they sent a Belizean Army patrol down the river to have a look. According to a survivor, a 30mm opened up from the jungle and wiped out the whole boatload, our job is to go in and sort this lot out' Two land rovers of ten troops - sort this out. I see. We were thinking about that 30mm cannon pumping away into our paper thin land rover. Everyone was a bit worried, I started to think I should be too. 30mm guns were cool things in films when they opened up – usually atop a US tank as Telly Savalas takes on the Jerrys - 'cos they were on our side, but to face one spitting hellfire, without warning from jungle hideout? No thanks, and with that we all became a little pensive and serious in our checking of weapons, filling of ammo pouches, loading of magazines and oiling of weapons.

The land rover turned off into what can only be called a rich, lime green mass of lush overgrown one time footpath that we would quickly widen into a track by driving straight down the middle of it; any moment we expected to hear the crack of a giant 30mm bullet followed by arms and legs going missing. The high grass was forced down either side as our convoy made for what appeared as a village on the map. Suddenly we see a man walking down the path in a ragged clothes, a machete and a sombrero; he sees us, he stops. "Go for it' says the Major and the driver floors the throttle as Mister Sombrero turns and scarpers, we hang on as both land rovers roar down the track at 40 mile an hour and we in the back on the ramp hang on to the vehicle and our cocked weapons, I look at my smoke grenades, ready to prove to the snotty major that I can lay down some formidable smoke, whether he wants it or not. We keep driving - but the guy's disappeared; could this be an ambush? Will we discover a welcoming ceremony consisting of a man sat atop a half-track with his prized possession of that 30mm? Let's face it you can't really get wounded by a shell that big– it just tends to take half your body with it.

Grass became jungle, it got darker, became a village of rough huts made of grass, sticks, leaf, and villagers going about their business – and then I realise - there's no men; just women and children and definitely no sign of the running man as we slowly discover one of our Land Rovers has blown its clutch.

The villagers know nothing about any drugs. It looks like one of those Vietnam villages before it gets torched, which makes me all the more aware that I am casually walking about armed like Robert de Niro in The Deerhunter; the villagers clearly haven't seen this film lately and seem pretty calm about us wandering about with guns sticking out of every available orifice. The interpreter chats with the locals and the Major, whilst I begin to think that perhaps I might survive the day as we limp out of the village and start looking for where in this Turkish sauna we're going to spend the night. I pull a cord between two trees and set up my hammock, stretch a mosquito net over the top and a waterproof smock over that, with my rifle doubling as a pillow and an efficient divider for the two sides of the hammock that I lay my head on, a stiff stick doing the job the other end down by the feet, all of us aiming to get the whole thing at least five feet off the ground to avoid all the nasty snakes that could outrun you, giant spiders that could your face, let alone the gorillas, leopards and various monsters we kept hearing stories about.

'Everything here either wants to shit on you, bite you, or spit at you' said the soothsayer in the team.

The translator turns up and hands round a few minute peppers he'd got from the villagers to stir into our compo' rations, the paras seemed to know all about these

'Go easy – these are Habanero peppers.'

I gingerly diced and added one to my chicken curry. Yes, I guess I used too much. I should have known, the villagers probably gave them out as a concealed weapon, for under the jungle canopy my internal temperature rose to virtual incineration point as my pores exploded with sweat and I lay pondering my reasoning in choosing chicken curry with extra pepper whilst sleeping in the midst of the Belizean jungle. I tried to lay under my mossy net, what felt like the midst of running a marathon, thinking about snakes crawling up the tree and then somehow falling on me - just as darkness shut out the light with the speed of a safe door closing. My turn on sentry duty was at 3am and for once I actually looked forward to it, I could at least get some rest then. Little did I know that my biggest worry was to come from the soldier I'd be guarding with.

3am. I'm nudged out of my hammock in the blackness by what I presume is the off-going Para and I manage to find myself standing next to a Corporal - I can't really see him and we're gazing into the black jungle as he reveals in a moment of reverie that he wants to be a postman; he's done his three years, fought in the Falklands and wants no more to do with the Army. Guess he's seen it and done it. Most of these guys were pretty talkative and human once you got below the exterior, and I thought it funny how this job forces you into these strange encounters; but hang on, a Postman? The very opposite of a fire breathing Para; maybe it's true what they say, those who've seen real action don't want to talk about it and don't want to relive it.

But suddenly we're both startled by a roar of something very scary. A blood curdling roar that echoes through the jungle.

'Lion.' Says the Corporal in the blackness.

63

'They haven't got Lions in Belize – have they?

'Tiger then.'

It roars again. Closer, scarier than before, we both wish we'd read up on wild animals in Central America.

'Don't think they have Tigers.'

Another roar comes from the other side of us – a few hundred metres away.

'Whatever it is there's two of them now.

Another roar - from somewhere else.

'Three'.

The roaring gets closer.

'They're closing in'.

'Fuck this' He cocks his weapon.

'Erm -m hang on - I think there's troops asleep out there – somewhere.' Imagining him suddenly unleashing semi-automatic fire and taking half our platoon with it in the process of fending off three Tigers. I hear him lower the rifle, I think – I dunno because I can't see a thing. But the roars are bloody scary; like out for your blood scary. For the moment they stay about a hundred metres away, in a triangle with us at the centre, shouting at each other. We're terrified, clutching our rifles like boy scouts with pea shooters. Could have been worse, could have been asleep in my hammock.

'Howler monkeys' says the interpreter next morning after we've told the camp we'd defended them from ferocious Bengal

Tigers who'd somehow swum to Belize. We nod sheepishly whilst I check my smoke grenades, the Major continues his look of disgust. What is it about me and Parachute Regiment Majors?

But the second day dawns as fast as the sun sets and we're off to have a look for more drugs – with one being towed as a sort of 'bait' into the staunchly 'pacifist' Mennonite community. Talk about contrasts - the farmers wear straw hats, the women dress in Gingham check and cover their heads from the sun by wearing Oklahoma-style bonnets Not surprisingly, as our travelling circus of heavily armed bandits arrives they regard us with indifference – the women look as if the devil has just arrived - and admittedly these were the 'red devils'; they also don't believe in TV or telephones, and looking back I think their reaction was a considered, intelligent response rather than one of naïve shock - they knew all about people with guns in this part of the world; they'd chosen to avoid all that and rode around in horses and carts with dungarees. And here we come, stumbling through with just about everything they had cast aside... looking back I sensed they were respected by the local population.

We were quickly in open farming land with the odd homestead but suddenly we're looking at a windsock in a Mennonite farmer's back field. We pull up, out comes the farmer with requisite straw hat and dungarees, mid fifties, easy-going. 'Why the windsock'? Asks the Major through the interpreter. Farmer replies that it's just for decoration, but when asked about reports of planes arriving, without blinking he replies that 'yeah, planes sometimes arrive but they have nothing to do with me.' The Major murmurs over his shoulder to his Sergeant that this is just like Northern Ireland all over again; locals spinning yarns when there's a pretty strong clue he's allowing drug running aircraft to use an airstrip out the back of his field, but despite the chance of a stake out and drugs bust of a sneaky drug running Cessna, the towed land rover is becoming a problem, we're getting nowhere here, and we need to go home.

I see my first Tarantula spider as we climb over a fence, making its way along the track in front of me; I bend down to have a look, but a boot comes down very purposefully crushes it into the mud; the smiling interpreter looks at me, shakes his head. I watch the spider slowly lift each limb out of the mud, then carry on his way. Nature out here is ruthless, hard as nails and unstoppable.

On the way back I listen to the conversation of the Paras; the Major is in the other vehicle out of earshot; I ride up front with the driver and he talks of 'crap hats' like me - shortened to 'hats' meaning everyone who's not a Para; the sense of superiority is very clear, yet they're all perfectly civil to me, then again I guess I'm beneath the radar, like I've momentarily made friends with a wild dog. It was hard not to feel a certain sense of envy with this team though; they may be tired and whiny like any other unit, but there was an undoubted instinctive trust and knowledge of each other's capabilities which they couldn't apply to us two RAF regiment squaddies in their midst, so we were kept at arm's length, especially by the Major.

Although as RAF members we were largely ignored, other Army units on the base suffered – a few days later someone is stabbed with a chisel on Airborne Forces celebration day and the paras are shaven headed and given a forced march as punishment – they came back forty eight hours later with a proud look on their faces.   I remember trying to drive a land rover on a supply run through the drunken mayhem that was the evening celebration - Paras littered the campus like you'd driven into the wrong ghetto, looking as if to block the land rover; we increased speed and they grudgingly stepped aside, narrowly missing them.

So, no 30mm, no drugs bust, no gunfight; we disrupted a native village, scared the Mennonite community and stuck our noses into the Belizean way of life; which was working just fine without us. But I loved the place so much I went back there for my holidays, intrigued with such a range of people that would wave as you arrived from the airport - just out of pure friendliness.   To think I didn't want to go on this posting, it remains one of the highlights of my life and proof that within a year of my biggest failure (parachuting) I was having one of my most memorable experiences; I guess we can't always plan success and experience.

Looking back I almost can't believe I was on that patrol and I never used the twin smoke grenades and never let off a round in anger – not even at a Howler monkey. As far as I know the drug running continues just the same as before.

Chapter 11

I discover a mountain in a waste tip

I'm shuffling my feet, killing time by a small rubbish dump, which backs on to a barbed wire fence – holding a loaded rifle, standing sentry.

Killing time is right - I'm in the RAF Regiment, shamed and written off. As a potential paratrooper I made the rather impractical discovery that I was petrified of jumping from a balloon whilst on the jump course - I was unceremoniously thrown out of the elite para' unit and transferred - to here. Guarding a rifle range on the outskirts of Dundee.   Here I am forced to re-assess my suitability for RAF pilot as I shuffle about on the edge of a waste dump.

It's 1983, Human League and Spandau Ballet are still ruling the charts, pastel suits and easy money are coursing through the streets of Soho and I'm twenty-one years old, deflated, lost, hanging about with an unloaded rifle standing by a tip. Talk about a level of pointlessness hitherto I'd not come across before. Some old geezer wanders up for a chat and tells me something about the place – apparently I'm next to a famous golf course called Carnoustie. But despite this information, two hours standing here, on my own, whilst the lads shoot everything they can find at the wooden targets a few miles away is not the most inspiring way of spending my day. I don't think there's any Russians interested in this range, and the IRA could choose much more significant targets.

I've already had my go – firing the infamous 88mm Carl Gustav Rocket Launcher - it's really impressive; I throw the launch tube over my shoulder whilst another loads the tank-busting missile, closes the rear tube and pats you on the shoulder with the word 'ready' then hunkers down to avoid the back blast; it looks like a scene from 'A Bridge too Far' with the Piat gun, just that this has more than a heavy spring to launch it. I squeeze the trigger and point at the knackered old tank about a 100 metres away; let's face it - it's big enough not to miss, but I'm expecting such a loud bang that I forget to look where it's going – 'whumpf' - off it goes I know not where - 'what the fuck was that?' says the bewildered Flight Sergeant as he looks at a smoking hole about thirty metres in front of us. Best I wasn't at Arnhem, and bang goes a lot of tax payer's money - your money. Sorry about that.

So back at the tip and here I am having to guard – against what? Not sure. Guess we've got weapons so we don't want anyone stealing them; but who in their right mind would attempt to sneak on to a rifle range whilst we're actually shooting at things with live ammo – and try to steal them? But here, in this unlikeliest of places, I make a discovery.

I kick through the pile of discarded tin cans and Reader's Digests. Surely from this place of pointlessness I can find something of value, of inspiration? Something to spur me on to better things? It's been nearly a year since I failed to do that parachute jump and since that time I've felt like the very asbestos beneath my DMS boots; an unwanted liability that is to be avoided at all costs. The Rapier unit don't do parachute jumps, or pack runs or unarmed combat or abseiling out of helicopters - in fact all the things I joined up for they don't do. It's a cushy number for some, but for me it was like an entire house had collapsed around me. I was still trying to let the dust settle.

I pick up one of the Reader's Digests and start leafing through. The only time I see these are in Doctors' surgeries and try to find the Humour in Uniform article, kicking over the pages without picking it up, but instead I come across a page showing a painting of a mountain called 'Popacatapetl' - something about a climbing trip to the summit. I read on, still leaving the page on the ground, looking down at the picture between my ambling back and forth sentry duty. Anyone else would have slung the rifle over the shoulder, picked up the magazine and started reading- but I hang on to my training and still won't accept I'm one of *those* guards. I took the picture in - nothing could be further away from me. Here I am washed up, reading about epic expeditions to the top of the world; once upon a time I thought that'd be me. I pull out a squashed sausage sandwich leaking margarine and decide this is one of the best delicacies to be found in the country; the sort only a set of military kidney pouches could squash between ammunition and gun oil. As I munch I begin to consider this story; the fact that I still don't shoulder my rifle, that I still run, still have the need for ambition, and start thinking.

Ten years on. There it is, all 18,000 feet covered in heavy cloud and twenty miles away and I'm definitely NOT going up. I'm looking at it from the hotel window in Mexico City and to be perfectly frank I feel very similar to the day before the balloon jump. All you can see is a steeply ascending piece of land being sucked up into a giant thunderstorm cloud – Popacatapetl was somewhere in that cloud – it was actually scary just too even look at where it might be. The balloon jump was immediate - all or nothing - but what would be wrong with catching a bus to the foot of it? Like going up in the balloon cage and having a look - just a look? Tomorrow - I'd catch a bus to the village at the foot of it, hang about and then come home. I'd claim the weather was too bad – yes – who would know? It was Mexico – no one would know. I'll make one small step.

In the village square I sit looking at the cloud with my soon to be pointless mountain climbing gear and look around. I'll have some beans and rice before I head back –

'Hello mate – you going up the mountain?'

It's a rhetorical question really; I'm sat with ropes, crampons and a big rucksack.

'We're just over there – Army team – we're heading up to base camp in ten minutes if you want to join us.' I take another small step.

He explains they'd be acclimatizing for at least a week at 11,000 feet - to avoid altitude sickness (really? I nod in accordance as if that was obvious) and we make our introductions – Army doctor, Infantry officer and a woman army officer - along with a team of twenty odd men. Slowly I begin to realise this might happen. How can I back away now? In fact, why back away? You've suddenly got a team.   I hide my elation and decide to adopt the persona of the lone climber who does these things regularly without so much as a moment's fear. I take another step and jump in their wagon.

71

After a week at 6000 feet in the base hut, nearly all of us have gone down with altitude sickness – it's feels like your brain has been inflated and is sticking to the sides of your skull whilst some miniature bloke hits at the inside of it with a hammer. You want to drill a whole and let out the pressure, but I don't think that'll work. Nurofen works wonders, it's just that we soon run out and by the time we're ready for the climb there's just three of us up to it, and we decide on an Alpine start – 4am in darkness to try and make the remaining 7000' there and back in one day. So with banging heads like the hangover of hell we set out in the darkness and into that cloud. Making short steps forward because of the altitude, the three of us are collectively carried along by each other.

We all seem pretty fit, trudging along the worn stone path past hastily erected crosses where sulphur mine workers had met their end; it gets colder, steeper, then very steep. The snow arrives and we slow down even more. We break out the pick axes and the crampons, clipping them to our boots as the cloud starts to surround us and nature begins to gain the upper hand. Pretty soon the cloud has got thicker and we're starting to lose sight of each other, not only that it's white under foot and white above, there's no horizon, just white - what about the edge of the crater? What about this steep mountainside where crosses of dead people are scattered? We start to lose each other in the white out and decide to get out the rope and tie ourselves together at ten yard intervals. Crampons, roped up and ice axes; at last this was the real climbing I wanted to do; we all know the knots and tie ourselves off – somehow the casual professionalism of their roping up doesn't surprise me and we find ourselves trusting each other instinctively. But it gets even steeper and I'm beginning to struggle; the pungent smell of sulphur reminds me of wandering into an overpoweringly unclean public toilet – but here it's visibly pumping thick yellow smoke out of the gaps between the snow – like some underground toxic industrial waste site. It's uncanny to think this is natural – that somewhere up there in the cloud is a giant crater with active lava. Thanks, Reader's Digest.

It comes in waves; the pounding of the brain against the skull and I'm out of breath as the rope tightens and I force the guys to wait; and then ten minutes later it's me that's pushing on and waiting for the Doc' or the Infantry guy to catch their breath. We make our small steps gingerly along the crisp icy face, it begins to get treacherous as we cross the nearly vertically steep snow that could slip away at any time. Suddenly the cloud suddenly pulls back...

We're on the crater's edge with a two thousand foot drop below us, peering into a smokingly beautiful hell the size of a city.

There it is. My eyes cannot adjust. I have been looking in front of my nose for the last few hours at white-out and two blokes roped up to me. But suddenly I am being forced to stare out at a full sized gaping hole the size of Portsmouth - right at my feet. No one says anything. We couldn't. Whole clouds pass in front of us and block the horrifying view for a moment, and then slowly, wide eyed we watch as the crater yawns into view again. There you go, says nature, I'm here all the time if you look for me.

Piercing sunlight, air so clear and crisp you feel like your eyes have become super-sharp and nothing down there will ever really matter again.   The hole stays where it is – doesn't devour or attack or eat us whole. It just is. We take stock, walk along the rim, start the final few hours to the summit on the right hand side and yellow smoke is now everywhere like a poison gas attack – but the real problem is the altitude that saps your energy like an elastic band round your waist dragging you back down the slope. Five steps, pause, rest hand on knee, rope tightens, five steps, pause again. Deep breath - it's like someone is permanently farting in your face. Another five steps, maybe ten this time. Rest. The snow becomes ice as we skirt the side of the crater and start the final ascent through the rocky outcrops; we must be at 17500 feet, oxygen is normally needed in an aircraft after 10,000.   One, pant, step, gasp, at a time.

The cloud clears and the crisp clear air reveals a blue sky and the Volcano crater laid out far below us like some ideal but photo-shopped postcard. A couple are a few hundred metres in front and we can see a hut tethered by ropes, sat upon the uppermost edge of crater rim like a mythical wizard awaiting our arrival all these years. I think back to the rubbish dump, standing on guard at the rifle range, the Reader's Digest, this mountain summit being described. Here I am.

I think how I can have an idea – and make it happen. This is victory post parachute jump – in spite of it. I realise that anyone can make these things happen despite their past because I was the biggest failure in my own mind at the time. I let the tears come and blame it on the icy wind as I approach the hexagonal tin shelter. The steps come easier as we begin to run to the hut.

We hug, shake hands and make instant friends with the couple of guys - Germans - who are carrying nothing more than a day-sack on one of their backs compared to our giant rucksacks of bivi-bags, overnight gear and ropes. He opens it up and pulls out a couple of cans of lager and a saucepan. 'Have a drink!' He shouts, then looks at his crampons 'Do any of you know how to put these on?'

About a year later we met up for a celebratory meal in some Mexican Restaurant on the A30. Polite, well-mannered with wives and girlfriends; but what we saw and shared was beyond all this, there was a gaping hole in our conversation. But they were random, epic, mutually adventurous men who never spoke of being in the forces. To have shared such a special trip meant a lot to me, but I felt it was part of a long list of peaks to them. I guess I had other things to do.

But as I sipped that beer at 18,000 feet I'd like to have said how I suddenly thought back to the sausage sandwich moment by the rubbish tip in Carnoustie and the copy of the Reader's Digest that started this whole thing off. But it's not true, I was too busy getting my breath and wishing my mates were watching – knowing what this meant. Because what I did take away was far more powerful and not obvious to me at the time; given twenty years perspective; because what stands out for me was that you can take inspiration from anything – literally a rubbish heap at a time when I'd never felt more pathetic.

But far more important was the realisation that what seemed impossible can often be achieved by just a few tentative steps in the general direction - by all means be ready to turn back - but see what happens when you approach. Is there a brick wall? Smiling faces of deceit? Perhaps. Later for me that meant starting a degree, trying to teach, walking onstage for the first time; sometimes I met the equivalent of an Army team about to do the same thing and ready to back me up all the way...sometimes I didn't.   I never took that small step out of the balloon, but I think I've made up for it since.

Chapter 12

Goodbye Leuchars, hello to being called 'Mister'.

I came back from Belize and found myself losing a girlfriend (she had a fling with someone on the Isle of Wight, which resulted in me turning up in a trendy 80s bar that she'd gone to and doing the clichéd act of threatening everyone with a beer glass, followed by a quick ejection by a big bouncer with a plaster across his eyebrow) so, as predicted by the RAF, my relationship dwindled, I was now back in Scotland and wondering where my application to be a pilot had gone.

Where? Airmen weren't allowed to use the phone in those days, no emails, nothing. You can ask your flight commander but you need an appointment to see him, so you have no idea whether they're just laughing at you; turns out 2 squadron had lost it, so I went for a big run and shouted at the world moaning at the loss of a year when I thought my application was being 'processed'. A few more months and I have an interview on the base with two officers, one who corrects me for referring to my sixth form as 'college'; perish the thought that I'd gone to University! But they still seemed surprised that I'd got a few 'A' levels, was paying to fly at weekends and playing (badly) in the station basketball team.

I went for another run in the cold, bleak Scottish coastal area of Fife (I look back on it as beautiful, windswept and friendly), a Rover 3.5 pulls up, out leans one my flight commanders and beckons me over; he quotes German at me - something like 'Trim dicht funf mal vida' and I still, to this day, despite running it past many clever German friends, do not know what it means. I think it was something to do with 'keep trying and you'll get there' of course it might have been something highly philosophical like 'why bother', but it was a key moment of support for me. If you're out there Flight Lieutenant G from 27 squadron circa 1983, please let me know.

A month later I arrive at the aircrew selection tests at Biggin Hill (my third attendance, but first since joining the RAF). I wander into the airman's NAAFI and am immediately told that I was out of bounds by the squaddies, I figure it isn't worth explaining that I was still one of them, but already the change was beginning.

'Here's a question for you' said the RAF pilot behind the desk 'you didn't jump out of a balloon...' here we go, I thought, this is where it all falls apart and they accuse me of cowardice.

'So what makes you think you'll be able to eject if and when the time comes?'

I couldn't believe it. I expected 'so you're a coward, why should we have you as a pilot? Clearly you'll let us down in battle'; but no - a stupid question like this?

'I do think that my impending death in a jet heading at the ground would be an incentive to eject, much more so than willingly jumping out of a balloon when you're perfectly safe.' I may have shortened it somewhat but I was ready with 'have you ever jumped out of a balloon?' (Make sure they weren't ex-

RAF Regiment before asking) 'No?   Well how would you know?'
But I think they sensed I was about to bite their hands off,
something I lacked when coming from my comfortable home;
here I wanted this desperately, I was hungry, as they say.

A few weeks later and I'm walking back to the airmen's block in
my combats, floating on air. No more the camouflage fatigues,
no more the boots and puttees, no more the humping of heavy
green boxes, no more Leuchars, no more 27squadron. I'd got it.
I was going to be an officer. My two years as a squaddie had
worked. But I was still worried; I was confident of the flying bit,
I just thought they might kick me out for not being an 'officer'.

My social status immediately went up as I got in the car with the
head of the Mountain Rescue Team - he'd also been promoted.
We were both off to Cranwell to be made into officers and I'd
better start believing in myself. Would I make it? Would I be
able to hold conversations with Squadron Leaders? Would I
start threatening people with broken beer glasses?

Chapter 13

Cranwell and officer training

A guy is standing next to me with his puttees going half way up his leg, his beret looks like a helicopter landing pad and he has a gormless look on his face that in a moment, makes me realise that having a University degree doesn't make you universally clever. But he did have a degree, and yet here I was showing him how to put his puttees on correctly. Out marches our Flight Sergeant, he has parachute wings on his arm, he's ex-II squadron and I know I've had it - he'll know my history and he'll despise me. He does the usual shouting but addresses us as 'Gentlemen' and 'Mister'. He advises rather than orders us, he doesn't threaten us with missing weekends and squad runs and bull nights, and he just advises us how to do it correctly. I keep waiting for it to get bad, but it doesn't. Vindictiveness has gone for the moment, welcome to the world of being an Officer.

That night we have a 'Meet and Greet' with the executive officers; this will surely be my downfall, I'll be too shy to say a word and remain at the back like I always do in discos. But I found myself with Joan - an ex Corporal who would have been my senior last week and telling me what to do, now stood next to me, an equal, even more worried and nervous. We looked onto the open wooden floor where our flight commanders stood with glasses of red wine ready to mock and ignore. 'We've still got the room to clean, the boots to shine, the shirts to press' says Joan with a weary sense of 'why are we here', but I know this is important; 'Come on' I try to say with an impressive sense of bravado like someone about to make a bungee jump, and I lead her out onto the open floor in front of all the other nervous trainee officers, straight up to the lofty Flight Lieutenant, introducing myself and Joan as his new students. He nods, replies, the conversation takes off - It worked and I realised that if you are prepared to make that leap, the socialising was a mutual thing and would work - after competitive discos and balloon jumps this was nothing. I was later commended for being one of the first to break the ice, and Joan went on to become one of the highest ranking female officers in the Royal Air Force.

My first leadership exercise with ropes, pine poles and tyres had me adopting the approach of 'Attila the Hun' where no one gets a word in and I do all the talking. The RAF doesn't like it, even though I thought I was being a good leader by dominating everything and urging them all on; but what they wanted was someone listening to others, thinking, appointing a deputy and standing back to think. It didn't need to be hard; stand back and think. Great advice. It was also surprising to me that I wasn't expected to know this already, they told me and then expected me to put it into practise next time - which I did. It was almost as if they were on your side. I might get through this after all.

The fitness test; 'don't try too hard' all the other recruits would say - 'or else you won't show an improvement'; yeah right. I stormed off in the 1500 metres, beat the guy in spiked trainers who fancied his chances, and was left alone from there on. Whenever there was a PT run I'd be sent off to do my own thing, so of I'd go with a fellow long distance runner whilst the rest of the course suffered gymnasium beastings.

Some were kicked out for silly things like wearing brown shoes with the uniform, having the wrong haircut or wearing nylon shirts, but it'd be the cherry on the top, not the only thing they'd done wrong. I look back on Cranwell and Initial Officer Training as a bizarrely wonderful time where anything could happen; suddenly I was mixing with Oxford graduates who'd won sporting 'blues', Rugby captains who had trials for England but were committing to a career in the Air Force, things I was suggesting were being taken up, like a re-enactment of the quadrant race in Chariots of Fire which was a drunken challenge against the Rugby captain at midnight before our graduation. I found my previous history in the RAF, far from being mocked, was causing a certain level of respect from my colleagues for what I knew, which was another surprise. These colleagues on my flight, who were slightly younger than me, became amongst others, a decorated Group Captain and the other a Wing Commander managing the Red Arrows, yet here they were at eighteen, nineteen, Sean and Dave, just starting out - like me. I don't say this to impress, I want to convey the sense of wonder I have of hanging about with such capable people long before they became phenomenally successful, before they gathered rank and gold braid and disappeared up the corridor to the mahogany desk. It was good to see what qualities they possessed at that age, and it was impressive, the RAF chose well. But we'd head out to a disco in Lincoln and there'd I'd be as always, standing on the edge - Sean would say "I don't get it, you want to head to nightclubs but don't want to ask anyone to dance' sometimes nothing changes, the self-confidence obviously didn't extend that far. The Tony Manero/John

Travolta character from Saturday Night Fever is clearly still well beyond the levels of self-belief taught at Cranwell.

Eventually I managed to speak to my Flight Sergeant as he inspected my room; 'You probably remember me from II Squadron Flight Sergeant - the one that didn't jump'; he looked at me with surprise as if I'd told him it was raining outside, muttering something to the effect of 'big deal'. He thought of it as just another posting. He looked around my shining brass-work and pipes, shirts ironed, everything gleaming and turned to me 'it doesn't have to be Regiment standard here Mister Tallack'. And with that I realised I was off the hook, just pressing one sleeve of my shirts each night, leaving the rest in the wardrobe un-ironed. Once you'd proved yourself to the Flight Sergeant, they wouldn't close inspect you again. It began to dawn on me that I could do this. The things I thought were potentially going to get me kicked out I was perfectly capable of; socialising, conversation, being considerate - always things I'd been told off about and regarded as lacking in - these were easy qualities to adopt. On your own? No one to talk to at a gathering? Then attack the group of people standing there with an introduction - they all want to play the game and they'll let you in, very rare that they don't.

The tactical week was spent on Stanford Training area, which in the modern world of wikipedia one can discover as being where Dad's Army was filmed; for us it was a similar experience of running about playing soldiers, but a potential minefield for me since once again I was considered the battle hardened veteran, coming from the RAF Regiment; when it came to my lead I felt I was needing to prove something, make it look effortless or - something...

My mission was to gather information on the enemy - a kind of recce mission. I lead my team up to the edge of the enemy's camp in darkness, the WRAF officer following along, and decided it was best to show bravado and go straight in and see how far I'd get before having to shoot to blazes. Turned out to be absurdly lucky; we crept in with our faces blacked up and SLRs at the ready, but absolutely no one was in the camp, they were out setting up an ambush for us; so we went through all their kit, found out their orders and got out to await their return. Debrief was like my running record in PT, the WRAF officer was convinced I was an expert in tactical situations even though most of my experience had been rooted in the trenches of RAF Leuchars. But I was left alone after that. The real stumbling blocks came from where I least expected it.

Eighteen weeks I which we went from individual rooms in a barrack block to a halfway house mess with a parade square, finally to College Hall for the remaining six weeks where I suddenly found myself living in a place akin to St Pauls - both designed by Wren, walking to dinner in a suit and tie, wandering past original paintings of great air battles - the Lancaster attacking the Tirpitz, the Naval raid on Taranto - treading on the floorboard that creaked, walking past the Changi room, past the rotunda that no one was allowed to tread on until they were commissioned as an officer (and no one did - because we all bought into the rules of the club we wanted to join), and eventually into the dining room whereupon we were waited on as if we'd booked into a top class restaurant. It was like being in an elite public school, the difference being we'd all earned this position; 5 GCSEs, ability and determination had got us here, no parental money.

I ran every evening with Nasser, a future Qatari administration officer who was the same age but with three children. Quiet, humane and friendly, as we jogged along he taught me Arabic and we chatted of our futures. It was a special time for me, I was meeting such a varied range of people, having time to run, eating in style, playing a game which I wholeheartedly believed in.

My batman (assigned butler - to wash and press clothes and shine boots) had been Prince Charles', in fact someone would have had his room; what with the wide corridors, oak walls and marching in front of this stunning architecture, one felt a meteoric rise in confidence, standing, self-worth. It felt like hallowed ground that would never be altered, as if we would live in College Hall for the rest of our careers. Until I turned up for dinner at my Flight Commander's House...

His wife was an excellent conversationalist, always keeping it going despite our nerves and lack of subject matter; and that night, being the eighties, was fondue evening. We dutifully dipped our meat in and enjoyed the novelty of middle class behaviour; but unfortunately the flame had gone out under the pot, and I kept dipping in the lamb and chewing away oblivious to the fact I was eating uncooked meat. It was my turn to write the 'thank you' note to deliver to the Flight Commander's house my next morning, but I was too busy being sick into my sink. Parade was at 8am next morning...

I somehow made it down the stairs in uniform and stood on parade in front of the Flight Sergeant on the verge of being sick - I'd seen it happen to Regiment guys after a night's drinking - but not here. The Flight marched up to me and took one look at my face 'and that is what happens when you cannot hold your drink'. Dammit, falsely accused - it was the lamb! Followed by the Flight Commander's briefing with which he ended with the bombshell: 'Incidentally, it is good manners to have the thank you note arrive the morning after the evening; it's too late now - the damage has been done'. All eyes looked at me. It was the bloody lamb.

Eventually the pass out - or graduation - came and I was one of the guard commanders who marched along with an incredibly expensive sword in front of Princess Anne. My parents and ex-girlfriend came - more of a friend I guess - now - though neither quite knew what we felt about each other. I was never to see my fellow flight members again apart from Dave - destined for Linton on Ouse and basic flying training. The rest went to the four corners of Administration Officer, Catering Officer, Engineering Officer; the rest of us were aircrew - a boyish crowd of alpha males hell bent on the competition to become fast jet pilots; looking back we just looked naïve to be honest - as if we thought ourselves worthy of being jet pilots even though none of us had even tried it yet. It was the older, potential administration officers who provided more humanity, more conversation outside of flying, more breadth of horizon and experience.

We tore our white bands of our caps and were immediately officers; walking back to our parent's cars airmen would salute us for the first time and we, slightly embarrassed, returned the salute in front of our approving parents. Silly really, but the last eighteen weeks had been a significant step for me. A silly game had been played, I'd joined in, worn the right clothes and made the right decisions, and I was just left with the fun bit - flying training. Hang on, hadn't I felt the same about parachute training?

Chapter 14

Follow that wingtip

Dull overcast. Thick, low cloud that says it's not a good day to fly. Met briefing at 0800; we troop into the neon lit hall and slump down in the green nylon covered chairs, up comes the UHP display and the met-man shows us isobars and pressure drops and cold fronts, but it all says the cloud tops are five grand so maybe we can get that three ship formation trip in after all? So, although outside it feels all wrong, a day when the toast and jam in the crew room beckons, the brief tells us there's work to be done.

Outside the rest of the world are on their way into work, queuing up on the outskirts of York, another day at the office just like I was doing in Fareham back at the Unemployment Benefit Office three years ago; but right now I'm strapping in, stowing the eight ejector seat pins and running through the pre-start checks as my instructor straps in next door, rain is spattering our visors and I press the button that coolly drives the canopy shut.

I press the start button. Unlike a racing car, or a powerful motorbike, nothing springs into life, instead you get a slowly developing whine similar to an electric kettle starting to heat up, you can just hear it as you watch the gauges jump off their stops and start registering jet-pipe temperature, oil pressure, right way up (artificial horizon). Check in with the other aircraft, taxi out to the holding point, check the engine, line-up on the runway with the other two.

We sit there on the wet, black tarmac. Our breathing is forcing its way through the intercom and my left hand is sat on the throttle lever awaiting the takeoff clearance.

'Bravo formation clear take off'

All three jets quietly slide out and into the shape of a 'V' on the runway, just like we briefed back in the crew room. Touch of brakes, back on the throttle, hold on brakes, I'm staring across my instructor and into the cockpit of the lead aircraft diagonally to my right, he looks over at me. Full power, the needles spin round to their stops, I push forward against my straps to check I'm strapped in. I give the eject brief, my instructor nods and says he's got it. We sit there, full power, waiting. Straining.

'Rolling'.

The lead jumps off his brakes and I'm right with him, holding myself at his wing tip, I start to catch up, a little back on the throttle, not too much, I'm supposed to be taking off so I need to keep the power on, at the same time not bumping into the wing of the leader, white lines are rushing by out the corner of my eye as I watch the lead and keep that red and white wingtip just yards away. It bounces, it's lighter than air, flying speed, as one the three aircraft reach take off speed at the same time. I dart across at my gauges and check the Air Speed Indicator – take off speed – ease back on stick - she's off.

'Keep your eye on that wingtip'

Draw a line between the lead aircraft's left wingtip and the nose of his aircraft – keep it constant and don't let it vary – you move down that line as you move closer and closer to the lead aircraft, until you're just feet away, even though the lead's bouncing up and down in turbulence and you haven't time to watch the ground, or clouds or enjoy the view, you're riveted to that line between the wingtip and his nose and keeping your aircraft on that line, jogging around next to his nav light; if you touch you'll lose a wing, pull the handle, eject... it would be very embarrassing, you realise it's fun but actually bloody dangerous, you're sweating as you work and then it goes dark... you've entered the low stratus cloud.

You can still see the other two aircraft on your wingtip, their red rotating lights start to reflect off the inside of the cloud producing a weird sense of a strobe in a disco, but if you lose them then get the hell out of there, no one wants another aircraft belting through a cloud a few feet away if you can't see each other, so you keep close, watching that wingtip, watching that nose, glance at the speed. It's said if the formation leader flies into the ground you follow him - obviously not - but that's how close you have to be watching him, you just trust he isn't about to stall or fly into a cliff face.

Suddenly, we punch out of the cloud tops as if entering a new universe, a universe where a powdery early morning dawn bathes the cloud-tops gold and glints off the other jets' underbellies and we're in the world of the few; it's a sky like those holiday evenings in Cornwall when just a moment ago I was down there with the rest of the world, amongst the cars and the Monday and the cloud and the drizzle and now here we are, skimming the cotton wool and still climbing, red lights turning, wing tip to wing tip, just our breathing and the dull whine of the Rolls Royce Viper as I jockey the throttle trying to keep the leader's nose in line with his wingtip; the early sun's shadows travel across the cockpit as I try to concentrate...

'Look at that - beautiful'

'Yeah - keep your eye on the wing tip'.

Nothing else matters, we are locked into formation and my actions are instinctive; every miniscule movement of my arms are keeping my plane in that exact position - the sky revolves around us as I begin to be aware we are in a steep turn, it doesn't matter, all my actions are in unison with the leader. My eyes are on that wingtip, nowhere else. Someone said it's dangerous, and I guess if I did hit that wing I could easily take it off - or take mine off - the combined movement is slow but the momentum behind us is pretty well unstoppable. Best forget about that - get closer - closer. Back off the throttle - too much - bit more. There was no doubt, as we skimmed those cloud tops in 'V' formation and climbed into the clear blue yonder to practice tail-chasing, this was one of the most beautiful moments of my life so far.

'Line astern - go.'

We levelled off and I steered the jet into line astern, putting my canopy so close to the jet pipe of the leader's aircraft in front that if I'd have pulled back a little the nose would have nudged the tail of his aircraft. Whenever my nose rose too high his jet exhaust blasted into our canopy and buffeted the windshield with 400 mph of hot exhaust gas. So I edged forward on the stick, kept rocking the throttle to stay right behind him, too much throttle, pull back, drifting away, push throttle forward, edge closer, too close, pull back, push forward, heavy breathing, man I'm using a lot of fuel.

'Tail chase - tail chase - go' and with that he dives away as I try to follow in a mock dogfight, at times I didn't know whether I was diving at the ground or pointing straight up, I was riveted to the red and white jet ahead like we were playing some playground game of tag - how on earth was I getting paid for this? I was combining the movements of my feet and arms just trying to stay behind the jet in front as he rolled to the right, looped, pulled up, stall turned, rolled to the left. It was a perfect world, total freedom, something you'd find on a video game but I was sweating, puffing, heaving, breathing, forcing the breath out as the 'G' pulled my cheeks back and we chased each other around the timeless, limitless world above the stratus far below, far below on this weekday morning. I didn't want it to end.

'Check bingo'

We all checked our fuel state and called back our individual readings.

'Roger - line astern for recovery - go'.

As briefed we formed up on his left wing tip with me as number two, I felt my hand pulling back on the throttle to stay with him as he brought the speed back and began to point the nose at the cloud, but I was entering blind - just trusting the leader as suddenly we punched at 400 miles per hour into the wisps and then the thick greyish white-out. I'm not on instruments, I'm not the one following radar headings, there could be a big hill in front of me - I have to trust the leader and keep on his wingtip. The cloud gets thicker, I can't see his nose any more , just the revolving red light of his port navigation beacon ten feet away, if I lose him now I've got problems because there's someone on my left wingtip and he's relying on me...

'Bravo formation check in'

'Bravo One' I reply, quickly followed by 'bravo two' on my left.

'Bravo formation on the rejoin for run and break'.

The throttle goes forward as the leader inches away from me, the speed steadily increases and we begin to glimpse land peering through the bottom of the cloud, the cloud eventually lifts above the rotating beacon and all I see in the periphery is green fields getting closer and closer - but the red beacon still turns and I edge of my aircraft to line up that nose and wingtip. We skim the ground as we bounce along in echelon port, sweeping past trees, buildings, cows, roads, there could be a brick wall in front for all I knew but they all flashed past just like those golden cloud tops as we descended to 500 feet, now the world really is rushing past but it's like I'm a passenger as I can't see what's coming. I must keep the leader exactly there - they'd be watching from the crew room now as the formation roars over the runway yet to us there's just a strange bouncing and bobbing of metal - like boats at sea in a line.

'Bravo formation for the break'

'Roger Bravo formation you are clear run and break - call finals.

'Roger'

The most beautiful scene I have ever been a part of is about to occur.

My leader suddenly hauls his aircraft to the right and up and I am suddenly presented with a plan view of the underside of the

Jet Provost with all its roundels, red wingtips and jet pipe before it suddenly disappears into a steep arching right turn and he's gone - leaving me hurtling in a straight line towards oblivion. I count...

One, two, three.

Yank the stick to the right and pull, at the same time close the throttle, pull - pull check the speed decreasing - there's the leader suddenly a mile ahead of me with his gear down and turning finals. Speed drops through 125 - drop the gear - throttle up - drop the flaps - pre-landing checks - three greens - done - turn finals - little bit of power - 'bravo two on the break' - 'roger bravo two clear land' 'roger bravo two clear land' - full flap on finals - speed decreasing to 115 over the threshold - bump - we're down and bravo three is still behind me so keep the speed up and taxi off out of his way.

It's called a run and break and it's used to get fighters down quickly in wartime and so minimise the time they're at slow speed and vulnerable.

We taxi in, line astern, park up.

It's a dull day as we walk back across the tarmac, the drizzle continues, check in the aircraft, debrief, toast and jam in the crew-room. The rest of the day is strange because normally people want to get away from work and start living their life from 5pm. Here life only existed whilst you were working, everything else is just waiting to get up there again. Tomorrow would be more formation, more tail chasing, more run and breaks.

Times like this I couldn't wait to go to work.

Chapter 15

Heroes, survivors and friendly farmers

I'm bobbing up and down in a one-man dinghy in the middle of the North Sea. There's about fifteen of us all bobbing up and down in our little miniature life-rafts complete with little flashing beacon, blow up canopy and internal bailer – a plastic scoop to stop the thing from sinking. It was good fun for the first hour. Then you start feeling sea-sick.

A few hours later. You're cold, sick, shivering, sinking. Bobbing up and down.

Suddenly you hear the thumping sound. It gets louder. Deeper. A yellow speck. You've been waiting, hallucinating so long for this. You make out something dragging along below it. A man. Skiing. No. Surely not.

The man is suspended below the chopper, making hand signals to the pilot above.

He's skidding along the waves of the North Sea on his knees. He's coming straight for you. He's a hero, your best teacher, your favourite uncle, a move star, you name it – all rolled into one because he's coming straight for you to take you out of this hell.

Hiya mate!

Crash, water. A mass of parachute lines, dinghy chords and assorted tangled chords and you don't know what's going on and what's this?

'Alright mate just relax here we go.'

Somehow amidst this chaos he's cut all the right lines and connected me to the harness and here we are floating out of the sea and up and up and – into the padded noise of the Sea King. He disconnects and is off again to get another. I look around at the shivering fellow student pilots and realise we've just discovered a hero – the helicopter winchman.

But this is just the start of our survival exercise.   Still soaking we were ditched in a wood somewhere in Yorkshire and had to catch and survive for a about a week. That 'about' was going to become annoying. But down to work. Traps, trip wire, I made a particularly good bow and set of arrows. I was Robinson Crusoe, this was easy. We could do this forever! Next challenge please...

Four days later I've set my traps, made a tent out of my parachute and am reduced to boiling fern stems in my tobacco tin which doubles as a saucepan over a fire I lit from magnesium, silver birch and assorted kindling.

And I'm starving hungry.

Our survival skills are that good, none of us have eaten for four days - such is the quality of our rabbit traps. In between being messed about by the bloody survival instructor on the wet and windy North York Moors the lack of food has made us all particularly lethargic and lazy. There's no energy to do anything.

The idea is to make us all able to fend for ourselves in the wild, but I soon noticed that the powers that be keep rounding us up to do silly energy sapping exercises; like retrieving a downed airman from a tree (dummy mannequin stuck in some branches), or killing a domestic rabbit bought from a local pet shop and trying to barbecue it.

So I realise the best idea is to get away and start setting traps and trying to fish using the odd worm – I'd already tried cooking them but they tasted like elastic bands. So there I am, sat by some babbling brook amongst the hills of Yorkshire wondering how the RAF find a place so desolate in the midst of England, when all of a sudden this tractor pulls up.

'You on one of them survival exercises I bet'.

'Yep – sure are'.

'I bet you'd be in need of a bit of food then'.

'Oh yeah – just can't catch anything'.

We all know the locals are under strict instructions not to feed us and it's supposed to be a simulated survival situation behind enemy lines – so I shouldn't be hanging about in the open really.

'So you wouldn't mind some potatoes and the like?'

'Ah that's okay – we've got to catch the food – exercise and all that...'

Now this may sound stupid to you – refusing a gift of food – but that was me, if it didn't fit with the plan – well then.

The farmer looked non-plussed;

'Oh well, I'll leave 'em by the gate if you feel like them later'.

I wandered back to the camp – the trainee pilots were staggering about on some bloody map reading task and hadn't been able to find me.

'Never guess what guys – been offered food by a farmer.' Suddenly, I have the instant and total attention of fifteen wannabe pilots who want to know where I hid it. Bear in mind such was our hunger the thought of twenty odd raw potatoes was equivalent to the promise of a night at the Ivy.

'I turned him down'.

'You what?'

'Turned him down'.

'You mad?'

I was genuinely surprised – surely it was cheating? Our mission was to capture food not take it from the farmer. I had a lot to learn.

I mentioned he said something about leaving it by the gate, and with that our most lethargic of students was hot-footing away and turned up with a furtive look on his face two hours later. He'd stashed the booty on the edge of our camp and that night he and the others were planning a secret midnight nosh-up. Potatoes. Raw.

Needless to say we were attacked that night and had to 'crash bivis'; that is, pull your makeshift tent down and run for the hills to evade capture. We ended up trying to erect our parachutes using available twigs and para-chord in teeming rain at 2am. I still managed a fire and some boiled fern – apparently it was this madness in the face of poor weather that got me a good report from the instructors. However, looking back. The saner amongst us – as in the guy who'd stashed the food, then marched back the ten miles or so on his own to find that plastic bin liner of left over potatoes - made a lot more sense.

After seven days we were finally thrown our first food – carrot pie - yet my stomach was so shrunken I couldn't eat more than one helping, even though later over the weekend we'd fill ourselves to bursting with pizza, that first carrot pie was the best.

But I came away with an urge to make a fire from nothing but silver birch, to erect a tent from my recently ejected parachute, to set traps for rabbits and boil fern stems. But I've never had the need. You can't do this for fun, yet if you're doing it for real something very bad has happened - shame really.

PS: In a later exercise in Wales I suffered my own instructor landing a punch to my stomach whilst I had a sack over my head that I won't forget; 'Resistance to Interrogation' they called it. It was then I nicked the mars bar off the front seat of the land rover - without guilt - and realised the rules had changed.

Chapter 16

Close call

I'm pulling 5G in the turn and the sweat is popping out of my forehead and forcing its way out from the helmet and down my nose as I hang on, pulling the jet through a 270 degree turn with the trees spinning past underneath. At 300 knots, I trace the turning point with my wingtip and scan the vertical horizon as my compass edges round onto the next heading. Suddenly into my vision there appears the black silhouettes of what we call 'sport'. Two American Tank-Buster ground attack jets, over the North York Moors they're a legitimate target and I shove the throttle to max-chat and go hell for leather in pursuit to get on their tail and claim a 'kill' – 'fox two' as they say – I was already preparing my 'you weren't watching guys' as I sneak up behind the Yanks …

But they clearly *were* watching as they suddenly sling their madly capable airframes into a 'shackle' manoeuvre with one twisting to the left and one twisting to the right – their rate of turn far surpassing mine and leaving me floundering at low level going full throttle, five miles a minute into the wilderness somewhere south of Malton with two suddenly disappeared A10s probably rapidly coming round onto my tail. Lost 'em.

Hurtling along at this relatively high speed unsure of your position can be very embarrassing if you've got a radar no-go zone four miles away and several congested air traffic zones in the area and with all this excitement and low level throwing about I had naturally forgot to check where the hell I was for thirty seconds – somewhere in the Vale of York I had no doubt, but how close to the radar site? I checked the map, momentary look down; not sure, still 300 knots and the absurdity of being in command of her majesty's very expensive jet and yet being not quite sure what to do or where to take this heap of fast moving hardware was a somewhat curious predicament, though I didn't ponder this too long but instead scanned for some distinctive features – like Castle Howard or some such bloody great building...nothing. The whistling whine of the engine happily took me very quickly to wherever I pointed the nose, but I was rapidly running out of time and options and would need to get the hell out of there soon as I try to regain my track – which was somewhere out to the left; check map again - check stopwatch. My eyes linger over my kneepad map with its mass of roads, lines of pylons and notable landmarks – I look up....

There is a fan of sheep scattering in front of me – yes I mean *in front* of me. To say they were below is a little bit optimistic; some blades of grass, a tree with leaves, a line of bushes, all flash past and burn themselves into my memory as I rapidly, instinctively pull the stick back and roar skyward and into the safety of a cloud. It all happens rather quickly. Onto the radio, declare 'breaking out of low level requesting radar pick up and vectors for Linton on Ouse'. Soon I'm punching out of the cloud, levelling off and taking steers for base from the calm air trafficker who knows nothing of my near-death misdemeanour. The rest is automatic; descend on heading into cloud, line up with runway, stick the gear down, checks done, into land, back on the deck, taxi, sign the aircraft in, debrief with instructor 'got a bit lost near Malton, regained track...' wander back to the Mess, watch a bit of TV, have a bit of toast, read the papers, look into the fireplace, start contemplating… that was a flock of sheep in front of me… I didn't even want to think how close I'd come.

I was still gazing at the Telegraph in the comfy floral patterned armchair when Mark called me to the bar to regale me of his latest efforts at low level. I mentioned my near miss, it wasn't really heard, then a few others came in with stories of their own, all of which ended with their success and eventual victory over the odds. We were supposed to be steely blue- eyed heroes, not idiot chancers who get lost. It was Taranto night and the Navy students were firing bazooka cabbages across the bar. Oh well, best to forget all that and join in.

Chapter 17

Cheating (or really thorough route study)

Saturday: A long cycle ride from the station; out onto the moors and into the headwind, anyone watching would have wondered why this man was pedalling his old yellow racer to the small nondescript town of Barnard Castle in the midst of the windswept moors on a mid-winter wet weekend; it wasn't good cycling weather, but he continued down seemingly pointless lanes that went past nothing more than grain silos, an old church with a small lead lined steeple and a rather forgotten telephone box that bisected a crossroads.   Yet to him it appeared to be highly interesting stuff - what exactly was he doing?

Finally, after five miles or so he would be seen to pause and have a sandwich whilst taking a long look at a stone bridge – not that ancient but nonetheless of interest to this passer-by. After scribbling on a soggy notepad he set off, pedalling his trusty racer back to the station.

On Monday my red and white jet sailed at nothing more than two hundred and fifty feet across the north Yorkshire countryside, skimming across reservoirs and twisting through the dry stone walled valleys; to the farmer in his tractor, or the hiker pausing to look skyward it looked like someone was having going for a 'jolly' in an aerial sports car.

Inside the cockpit I kept up a running commentary: 'passing reservoir on our left – now – next heading two-two-zero degrees – fuel state four hundred above bingo and the next event is – crossroads in – 30 seconds.

'Okay you have just had a bird hit your canopy'

I pulled back on the stick and felt the G press down as we sailed upward and into the cloud, I could just about force out the words 'speed for height – check engine'.

'Your engine's fine' came the calm voice of the instructor again. Shut the throttle, attempt relight, point away from the town, radio call - mayday mayday...

'It has relit' came the instructor.

My rehearsed drills kicked into action: 'Okay – climb to five thousand feet and complete low speed handling check'. 'Right that'll do – that's the end of the drill - return to low level and complete your route'. And so I pushed the stick forward and the jet ballooned itself back amongst the trees and valleys. But already we'd covered another five miles whilst dealing with that little fastball. 'Where are you?'... 'Er – one mile left of track'. 'What are you going to do about it? 'Ten degree correction – no – I can see the IP' - 'then head for it'.

The Initial Point was a pylon crossing a road and I threw the plane into a sixty degree bank and pulled the machine onto the turning point. It was his final navigation test and missing one turning point would mean failure, back course, on review, confidence shattered and probable loss of flying career. A lot hung on the FNT – the most important part of which was this bit - the simulated bombing run. I fumbled with my maps - stowing the small scale map and retrieving the larger scale map of the five mile bombing run. Hit the IP on the right heading and the rest should come together.

'Now'

I punched the stopwatch and settled the machine at what looked like two fifty feet and five miles a minute. Trees flew past and sheep scattered beneath as I started reading from the Ordnance Survey map with one big line drawn down the centre of it. No computer, no GPS, just map, compass and the mark 1 eyeball.

'Five seconds silo on left – check'

The instructor noted the grain silo to his left.

'Fifteen seconds should be church without tower at edge of village on right - check.'

The small church disappeared under the nose but I was looking two miles ahead.

'Twenty seconds 'Telephone box should be at head of T junction two hundred left' - 'you'll be lucky' the squadron leader murmured through his intercom. Too small a feature to see at this height and speed, but then the instructor hadn't figured on me cycling the entire route the weekend before. The target should be appearing in the next ten or fifteen seconds.

'Tally phone box – left of track about one hundred metres that puts me one hundred metres left of track – adjusting right.

'Describe your target'.

'Target is in fifteen seconds - a bridge'

His eyes scanned the woods in front for any sign of a bridge – there was the clump to the left, there was the small farm – there were the pylons running in to the left – and there – yes there was the bridge.

'Tally – on the nose.'

I made a minor adjustment and the jet screamed directly over the target. Direct hit. 'Three span masonry with single track road - bombs away'. But no time to rest because here he comes again:

'Your engine is now beginning to clatter and you have a fire caption on your panel'

I pull her up again out of low level and up into the calm as I close the throttle. Flashing trees are suddenly replaced with momentary whiteout, then stationary clouds below and blue sky. Once again I call practise Mayday and get immediate directions for the nearest airfield whilst going the through the drill for relighting the engine. We recover for a practise emergency landing back at Linton on Ouse and bump back onto the tarmac in time for tea and cake. I pull the sweaty helmet off and wipe my forehead, not sure how to react to the incredulous reaction of the instructor.

How did I spot that telephone box – and the bridge? Three spans? Masonry?

'I gave you a bit of time to study the route by telling you the destination on Friday – but you must have spent all weekend planning that run in – such was the level of detail – well done. I don't recommend riding a bicycle over all potential bombing runs in future, it might give the game away; but for the needs of this course, to make sure I pass, why the heck not.

Chapter 18

Fast jets.

Yep, I got it. Ambition takes me even further away from habitation and onto the wilds of Anglesey Island, just down the road from Holyhead, where there's just one Chinese takeaway, an Indian and a local cinema from the 1940s showing one film, soon to close down.   Runs from the converted hospital of the Officer's Mess can be terrific, windblown affairs across sand dunes with the mountains of Snowdonia facing you across the Menai Strait, or they can be pretty well impossible as the rain from the Irish Sea lashes across the runway. Here I was, at RAF Valley, one step and six months away from getting my coveted 'wings'. It had been two years so far; two years with the two Daves, Mark, two Pauls, Chris, plus the Navy chaps destined for Sea Harriers, Ron and Steve. Things had gone well so far; people were saying I was one of the most likely to make it; determined, single minded, fit and always focused on flying.

But as one gets closer, I noticed that old vindictiveness creeping back in. It's as if the instructors are in their private club and how dare you try and enter our world?   We're gonna' do everything in our power to stop you. You get that feeling as you note certain changes; here you start wearing 'G' suits - tight, inflatable, rubberised bladders that sit round your mid-drift and legs and squeeze you like an iron fist whenever a valve senses you're pulling 'G' to stop you passing out; you also need an immersion suit because you're flying over the cold Irish sea - rubberised again with a rubber neck seal and rubber cuffs and a zip down the back like doing up a wet suit before you go surfing. You also need to wear warm clothing under all this because if you do eject you're gonna' need all the warmth you can lay your hands on. I thought I'd be clever by choosing a slightly larger immersion suit than the others because I wanted to feel like I had space inside to move around - which resulted in a really tight squeeze into the narrow Hawk cockpit - and a complete inability to move around.

By the time you had walked out to the aircraft you were sweating, by the time you got strapped in and did your checks, you were panting and felt like some Chinese Buddha statue; and by the time you took off and actually started flying you felt like you'd spent an unwashed weekend at Glastonbury - in other words, disgusting, without the opportunity for recreational drugs.

So I went up for a few flights with my ex-Phantom instructor, Martin; he seemed pretty decent; showed me the effects of controls, had a go at taking off and landing, which was much faster, but all going fine. First week done with the usual arsehole competitiveness of 'I've done a barrel roll' 'Really? Well I did the fastest circuit round the airfield'; but the bar was the best place to spot the vultures as they gathered around anyone stupid enough to confide in another trainee pilot that they might have had some difficulty with the initial mastery of a supersonic jet: 'Really? Slow round the finals turn? What else did he say? What did he give you as a mark? Really?' Followed by gossip to the very next guy in the bar 'so and so's for the chop...' You quickly learned not to express feelings or become the guy with the problem. If you start doing well again 'weren't you having problems last week?' Pretty soon I realised that this was just a bunch of guys continually boasting of what they'd done - they didn't care what *you'd* done - unless it was mess up - the important thing was that they'd flown a better finals turn, or flown a loop because they'd had so much spare time since they'd mastered the lesson so quickly, and with more style. Damn it got boring.

A few nasty rumours popped up; our senior course was just about to finish and there was a final aerobatics competition, two of the student pilots were in the running for the prize and one of them was told to tell the other that the competition was to be held tomorrow; so instead he takes him for a drink in the bar - they get 'wasted' - and at midnight he suddenly remembers to tell him about the aerobatics competition - and *he* hasn't been drinking...

One funny moment was when the Dining In night was due to take place - both the senior and junior courses were to dine with the instructors in full dress uniform with bow ties. Of course one thing I'd learned to do due to my fear of not making it as an officer at Cranwell was to tie a decent bow tie. Your average student pilot, straight from University or state school, hadn't bothered to master this and was consequently stuck when time came to dress up. There were no shops near to Valley to go and buy one on elastic and the RAF only issued you with the basis ribbon -untied. Suddenly I became the most sought after student by all the alpha male 'top guns' of both the senior and junior courses as a queue formed at my door - early twenty year olds, one who would become a future leader of the Red Arrows; future Tornado, Harrier and Phantom pilots were here, for a moment lined up at my door desperately needing my skill as I tried to yank the ribbon round their necks and stop

111

them from looking like a complete idiot. This takes me back to that chapter on the balloon jump and my marching the Special Forces group to the hanger to watch the return of the Falklands heroes. A moment when suddenly I'm indispensable with forces far greater than me - it's a weird thing.

The second week and suddenly things start to go wrong; the vultures were out and my steely eyed killer fighter jock character is being questioned - and self-confidence, that elusive quality that cannot be just bought, found, or worked at - starts to dwindle.

I squeeze into the cockpit of the RAF's Hawk jet trainer with my folds of immersion suit getting in the way as always, the smell of rubber sending me into the usual spasms of retching as I connect my rubber oxygen mask, pull through my rubber cuffs and stretch my dirty, stiff with dried sweat, kid leather aircrew gloves on and then connect my Personal Survival Pack connector to the life support system - this involves a valve that senses 'G' and so inflates the suit, an oxygen valve and the radio. I then take the pins out to arm the ejector seat and start going through the checks as my breathing starts coming through my headphones and making me sound like a panting caller on a sex phone line. Little electronic noises start making their warning sounds as I run through the electrical systems and start the engine. Meanwhile the instructor has hopped in the back in his properly fitted immersion suit, done his checks in thirty seconds and sat there counting the minutes whilst you eventually ask him 'your straps secure sir?' A punchy 'yep' comes straight back as he taps the dashboard in front and thinks about the fighters he could be flying if he didn't have to do this stupid job.   Flying instructors are not committed teachers, they're pissed off fighter pilots who've been creamed off because they're good; it also means they'll be the worse people to understand anyone who's having problems, they'll be the most impatient, the most bolshie, the most likely to chop someone and get angry with them if they don't instinctively 'get it' - because they did.   You imagine that in a secondary school? (Not all of them - some were darn good).

This time my instructor is someone different, and ordinarily I see no reason why I wouldn't get on with him - he seemed proficient, hardnosed, matter of fact, just like all the others I'd known; but the Hawk has swept wings and if you get low and slow on the finals turn you might just fall out the sky - and I treated the turn like a Jet Provost leisurely turning finals at something like 120 knots when you needed to be a bare minimum of something like 150 knots; but it was the reaction from the instructor that threw me, and spelt out my death knell. If only I'd known.

He screamed in the back cockpit, took control of the aircraft and went for it - shouting - completely losing control to the point where he must have been expecting me to throw my hands up in horror, but I thought to myself - this is a jet - you're flying it - put the power on and don't do that again - stay calm. Unfortunately this came out as a mocking of his shouting, which I have to say was part of the intention; but he was over the top, no matter how dangerous his reaction wasn't going to help anything. I flew another circuit, this time as he wanted it, still calm, but the dye was cast; we flew back, he told me to write my own report - which I did and made it quite complimentary - I could see no reason to do anything else. He grabbed it and ripped it up, clearly I'd messed up some major code of conduct here, ridiculed an instructor? As a teacher I can see how that must have felt, but I wasn't exactly laughing in his face whilst checking my mobile phone, or storming out the room. I was just trying not to react to the screaming and shouting - it was a jet, dammit.

So I get thrown someone who's been pre-briefed by my previous shouter. I try to shake hands but he's too busy, no introductions, it's my pre-solo check ride. Little did I know his nick-name was...

Chapter 19

'Wet leg' - I meet my nemesis.

'I hope you know your checks 'cos I'm in a fucking bad mood.'

That was the welcoming speech of my new flying instructor as I walked out for the pre-solo check ride on the Hawk jet trainer. I won't forget him.

Fat, bald, pissed off, like a badly abused Rottweiller with a Harrier patch on his upper arm worn like a cub scout's swimming badge. He stormed out to what seemed an enormous jet as if I was the passenger. I wasn't even sure if he was my instructor, the only way I discovered was when he got in the back seat – leaving the front ejector seat vacant for me to climb into.

It turns out he was called wet leg after pissing himself in a jet once. Suffice to say he had a grudge against me, and before all you pilots out there assign this story to the trash heap of 'yet another hard luck case of why I got chopped from fast jets' I will freely admit that I'd got low and slow on finals; but then again, I'd just started, and no one on that course was particularly breezing along. But never mind all that, the tale is worthy of reciting as a case on its own in terms of the sort of characters you meet and have to somehow 'get over' if you want to make it.

I was still fumbling over the checks – it was only about the fourth or fifth ride so we all found it a bit of a memory test to start with. But he was having none of it:

'Come on – what's keeping you – give it to me I'll start her up'.

The engine wound up and the dials flicked into life. I was thrown.

Right checks done - get her out of here'.

I struggled to catch up, it was like playing a piano; normally there's a set routine to this tune of flying a jet and my hands would work through the drill slowly but automatically, but throw the routine and I need to gather my bearings...

'What the fuck's keeping you – is this your pre-solo ride or what?'

Always we're told – if in doubt there's no doubt', 'always check', be safe, be sure...etc. Looking back I noted how some of the best pilots I flew with seemed to be the most ponderous, the most unaggressive, and the most friendly. That actually goes for most of the truly successful experts I've met in my life. So that's what I did – try to slow down. Of course this made old wet leg even more impatient. It was then I began to suspect...

Maybe, just maybe he was *trying* to make me fail. He took over the controls straight after take-off and sent the machine skyward over Snowdonia and up to 10,000 feet (blink of an eye) before putting the machine through his aerobatics routine – pulling 9G coming out of a loop, the sky swirled as he flung her from that into a barrel roll, a stall turn, Immellman, I just let him get on with it. I hung on – I knew what he was up to – so I willed myself not to get sick and not to black out - bear in mind this was supposed to be my pre-solo ride – I was supposed to be proving my ability by doing circuits, he was supposed to be checking me for flying accuracy, but I guess that could wait until he'd had his fun and stopped showing off. It left no real time for anything other than a practice forced landing back at base... so I wasn't surprised when he pulled the throttle back and gruffly spoke:

'Go on then – engine failure – you have control...'

I went into the drill for a Radar Practice Forced Landing – can't remember how it went but probably not that well, because all I can remember is his getting angrier and angrier. As we landed he stormed off – probably to tell his screaming mate that he'd got one over on me.

So I didn't go solo after that trip – instead I went on the slippery slope – we flew a few more trips – one to Stornoway where I confronted him and told him I wanted to change instructors because he was – an arsehole of the first order – which translated into (bearing in mind I was a 26 year old wanting to succeed) 'unnecessarily negative in his approach towards me. Funny how nowadays I'm far less polite, you'd think I'd have learnt some manners.   But instead he just looked at another American exchange instructor and said I'd just piss him off as well - so much for my transfer. The American wasn't sure how to react; Wet leg clearly had sway.   It was ironic because another student had just landed with his gear up at Stornoway – forgot to put it down – now that, surely, is worthy of 'pissing someone off'? But he went on to fly Phantoms.

Nope, I was diving steeply downhill with wet-leg and was consequently put on review with the section leader – had to fly

some trips with him. I was immediately allowed to go solo –
because it wasn't that hard – and things picked up whilst I just
flew with Wet Leg's boss; but all the time I knew I was 'on
review' – which means being 'looked at' – bear in mind the 'top
gun' philosophy of the jet pilot – an overwhelming self
confidence that truly thinks anything is within their grasp
(because it usually is – they are extraordinarily competent
people) – but the moment you suggest it isn't – that you can't
fly a plane like Douglas Bader – then that confidence takes a
pretty hard knock. It can be something that spirals out of
control and some of the high-flying jet jocks have never
encountered in their flying life.

My section leader was a nice guy; peaceful, considerate, calm.
Always shut his eyes when he talked – which prompted a few
jokes around the crew-room as to how on earth he must cope
with talking to ATC whilst actually flying. I flew about five
sorties and was back on course to get those coveted wings. In
the meantime we had a quick survival exercise in North Wales.

We were dumped in the mountains with nothing but a stolen
Mars bar from the front seat of a land rover. Myself and Dave
tried frying worms and eating bird's eggs before deciding they
were like elastic bands and the egg was probably a protected
species. After a few miles and nights tramping about the
mountains, we then had to meet up with certain 'resistance'
groups that would take us to safety on submission of a
password; but it was just a ruse to get us captured and start the
resistance to interrogation mid 80's style. I'm sure that
nowadays things are completely above board – unless you're in
Abu Ghraib...but for me I got a sack over my head and a well-
aimed punch to the stomach. I doubled over, winded,

118

unexpected. It was then I heard the voice. It did appear that good old Wet Leg had got himself in on the exercise.

Of course looking back on it I wish I'd just kicked him straight where it hurt most, pulled my hood off and followed through with a perfectly justified retaliation 'sorry sir - didn't realise it was you' hands tied or not, but once again, I'm 26, and I want to be a jet pilot...

So we came back from the exercise and I have just one final check ride with the Chief Instructor.   I should have been ready:

'Don't worry – it's just a confirmation trip'.

Good, should go like clockwork then. This is after I've been interviewed by some high ranker, who wanted to know why my scores had suddenly plummeted after flying with 'Wet Leg'. I told him. Didn't listen. I began to ponder if multi-engine pilots were quite such arseholes. A Hercules took off during lunchtime – I was beginning to envy the crew. Wet leg had never been near one...

So there I was flying with the Chief Instructor, blissfully unaware that no one flies with the Chief Instructor unless it's a 'chop ride'. Your last – unless you prove without any reasonable doubt that you are not guilty of Wet leg's reports.

So I flew my aero sequence over Snowdonia, I did some circuits, they all went well. The Chief closed the throttle and declared my engine had failed – what are you going to do? I radioed back to the airfield and came in for another of those radar practice forced landings.

I was a thousand feet too high above the airfield. No problem. I did a few 'S' turns and lost the height, just five hundred too

high on downwind, lost that too. Better than being too low –
and too slow (scream). Round I brought her onto finals –
correct height and landed her without problem. We walked
back to the crew room.

'I'll see you in my office in five minutes.'

I began to sense bad news.

I walked in and was met by the seated Chief and that high
ranker that had interviewed me before.

'I thought you started really well, aerobatics were good, circuits
– no real problems, and I thought to myself – why is this student
having to fly with me at all?'

He paused, probably sipped some water.

'But it was when I pulled the engine failure on you that things
seemed to go to pieces...'

What? Really? I replied that I was initially 'high' on my
approach – but did a good job getting her in safely – I'd
recovered. We all knew this was reasonable practice in flying –
don't lose your head and get her in any which way if necessary.
But I could see the resignation in his eyes – and the others –
they were decided... the report had been filed, I'd been on
review, that's it.

Suddenly my world collapsed. I could see things weren't going
to change. Wet leg must be listening at the door. The walls
were coming down. Five years of training. I was the keenest,
the idiot who stayed in at night learning checks, scoffed at by
the naturals who drank and got up to all sorts in the bar; when

there was me going for a run and learning my checks over and over. Tears began to well up. Oh no… surely not…

"I hope you're not going to cry…'

Shit. Even worse than failing the course, making a complete blubbering idiot of myself in front of seasoned Wing Commanders and Air Commodores. I performed a recovery worthy of a downhill skier on one leg doing the slalom and staying upright. I choked them back and concentrated for England and the RAF. Or what was left of them.

'Not at all. I'd like to enquire as to the possibilities of transferring to multi-engine – the Hercules to be exact.' A Herculean effort. I didn't blub.

The Wingco' stopped, surprised.

'I'd have thought you'd have been interested in helicopters?'

And maybe that would have been a good answer, but at the time all I could think about was getting out of that bloody rubber wetsuit and not having to fly with the likes of charmless air thugs like Wet Leg, ever again. No doubt he's working as Captain on some Airliner now - good luck to his crew.

'Can I just say that I'm really impressed by your ability to move on – to accept that fast jets are not for you and to reassess your options…'

I walked out – held on for thirty seconds – my life as I knew it since eleven was over – the last fifteen years of ambition stopped right now. So not surprisingly the tears well up, but it was going to be private, alone. I let them flow:

"How'd it go Loz?'

121

My fellow students were watching as I walked out sat in the corner...

I couldn't turn round, they knew why. Bugger. That was it, time to go, No goodbyes, I was too angry. I didn't expect it to happen here, not when I was quite enjoying the Hawk, even with all the rubber immersion suits and alpha-male crap in the bar, I could really do this, this wasn't hard. But the barrier had come from another angle, one of bitter, instant dislike, if only I'd known before wet leg wandered into the scene.

I packed and was gone.

Chapter 20

Aerobatics - at night

Whilst I was getting chopped for talking calmly to an irate instructor, mad things were going on with the course - the difference was that they were getting away with it.

You might remember Benny Hill and his little bald-headed sidekick when he is stopped by a policeman just as they were trying to rob a bank; 'excuse me sir could you tell me where you're going with that bag?' The sidekick replies 'Okay you've got me – we've robbed a bank and tied up the staff and were just about to make our getaway.' The Policeman looks nonplussed – 'oh, I was only going to caution you for parking on a double yellow'. Well I thought it was funny, and it almost happened again.

Instead of doing a solo navigation sortie, one student had headed straight down to his parent's in Exeter and aileron rolled over the house before nipping back with no one any the wiser. Great idea but Court Martial stuff and -yes you're quite right - tax payer's money. So a member of the senior course figured he'd also try something...

I'll tell it as a story, but it's more or less as I heard it.

'X', ran the throttle to the top left hand corner of the dimly glowing cockpit; full power. His first night solo - the hum of the engine behind him quickly became a juddering rumble as he held the Hawk jet on its brakes and watched the dials spin round to their position of take-off power. A quick scan of the numbers and all appeared at their correct position – all those hours of memorising made this scan second nature, time for the radio call:

Tango one five ready for take-off.

Tango one five is clear take off departing to the North West.

Roger one five – clear take off.

The brakes were off, his head and back pushed into the ejector seat like a Porsche on full throttle – the only difference was the acceleration after the first 100 mph – it kept coming and his back was pressed deeper into the seat but at the same time he had to keep his eye on the speed – 160 said the air speed indicator – time to ease back on the column, the rumble became a soft sense of floating as he punched the button above the throttle and felt the gear retract – the three lights turned from green to red to – out. The runway fell away and the coast swept past underneath. But all he could see were the lights of Bangor and the dotted lights of Snowdonia.

The moonlight cast a strange watery glow over the Snowdonia mountains as he passed 5000 feet – a few more seconds and the number 10 soon came into view.

Tango one five you are registering flight level one zero confirm?

Roger that one five – just conducting a low speed handling check at safe altitude.

He lied, he had other plans. With that he threw the jet into a steep dive and let the speed build – 500 – 550 – 600 – 620 – the transonic juddering began – 640 – shaking – 650 – he held on –

then smooth silence as the jet broke the sound barrier high above the mountains and the dotted lights of the Ogwen valley. Yes. Ambition number one complete.

He eased back on the throttle and let the speed decrease before throwing the jet into a beautiful loop – the lights of Bangor arched over his head, thin moonlit cloud flickered by as he kept pulling until he was level again – then a mere nudge of the stick sent the plane spinning to the left – he let the horizon spin around the moon before jerking it straight again, letting a chuckle out. Ambition number two – night time aerobatics. A few more ailerons rolls and barrel rolls and it was time for recovery.

It was as he was returning he noticed the flashing red light on his tail. Not his own – but one a mile or so behind.

Tango two zero requesting join.

That was his chief instructor's call-sign; what was he doing up here? It could only mean one thing - he'd been followed. He knew the chief sometimes shadowed students on their night navigation exercises just in case they got up to – well – mischief. That was it, career over, court martial, do not pass go, do not collect £200.

As the student taxied in he kept looking over his shoulder – there was the silent hawk behind him watching his every move. Suddenly the smooth surface of the runway gave way to the uneven rumble of the grassy verge – shit – he stamped on the wheel-brakes and jerked the aircraft back onto the line of blue lights that designated the peri-track. He glanced over his shoulder again – there he was – all he could see was the distant blinking red light and the silhouette of the chief's aircraft.

If you're just an airman and you do something wrong – like break a window or fail to salute an officer; you get a week's work in the cookhouse, perhaps a disciplinary hearing. If you're an officer it is officially 'high jinks' the overflow of exuberant spirit that defeated the Nazis in the Battle of Britain.

This, however, was beyond such reasoning; if there was a class difference then the forces love to play on that – but no airman flies – it is the realm of the officer and thereby 'high jinks' held no sway.

'Stay standing and keep your hat on.'

A bollocking always began with that statement. Here it comes, he thought.

The `Chief Instructor wore a huge moustache and said very little to students. Here he was in the inner sanctum of his office – the pictures of aircraft stared back at him; aircraft he would soon no longer have the chance to fly.

'What is the first rule of night flying?'

Honesty was the only way out – bite the bullet and take the posting to choppers – or out the Air Force. Best call up British Airways.

'Er – sorry sir - the first rule? Not to practice aero –'

'Sorry?'

Flight Lieutenant 'X' held back.

'Nothing sir'.

- Exactly – not to take your eyes off the peri-track lights when taxiing – you do realise the aircraft will have to be checked for any ingestion of foreign objects as a result of your lack of concentration – I was tailing you as you taxied in.

'Right sir. Sorry about that.'

'You're dismissed.'

'That's it sir?'

'What do you mean? Yes that's it – is there anything else I should know?'

'Er – no – nothing – sorry sir'.

'You see – there's nothing gets past me – always be watching your six.'

'Yes sir'.

He ended up flying Harriers.

Chapter 21

Aerobatics – really? – Again?

 So I had six months to go before my multi-engine conversion course began and I wasn't sure how I felt about that; to me it was 2 Squadron all over again; the failed balloon jump leading to work on the missile squadron. But I decided to fill in the gap with a stint flying Chipmunks at Teeside airport; they had room for a pilot to fly the Air Cadets around. It was here I was to find myself muttering to myself: 'Not aerobatics again'. Thirty years later teaching in a class five hours a day, I can't believe I said that.

I connect the rubber oxygen mask to my face and await the next Air Cadet to be strapped in to the cockpit behind me. A click and I hear the familiar, heavy nervous breathing of a thirteen year old scared to death but pushing themselves through peer pressure.

'And what would you like to do?' Through the spinning prop of the chugging Gypsy Major Mark 8 engine I check the bouncing gauges and I already know the answer:

'Aerobatics please sir.'

He can't see my face but I momentarily close my eyes and let out a silent sigh, not again. I've already performed a selection of loops, stall turns, barrel rolls and even a Canadian roll twice today – in two separate flights. I'm tired and have enough stories for an evening's entertainment in the bar, but here we are again with another Cadet...

I check out with ATC and clear for take-off, gently edging the Chipmunk left and right to check nothing's in front of the nose, because you can't see a thing with a tail dragger; that is, the aircraft has one wheel at the back, and two wheels at the front – and sits on them with its nose stuck up into the air – same as a Spitfire – which means you can't see a thing in front when you're on the ground.

'Okay, we'll take her up to four thousand feet, over towards Malton, then see what the cloud base is like.'

I volunteered to do this; 'Air Experience Flying' they call it, and when you've got a couple of months to waste because you've been chopped from fast jet flying, this is an ideal place to lick your wounds and remind yourself why the hell you got into this business in the first place.

Staffed by a friendly RAF Flight Lieutenant chap whose sole job was to take Cadets up into the sky four times a day and introduce them to flying; it was how I'd started and just about the most exciting thing I'd ever done at 13; to fly over the USS Nimitz aircraft carrier parked out in the Solent in WP 840 all those years back in 1974 – and then do aerobatics over the carrier! I still remember...

So here was I, Teeside airport, about to produce the same reaction in another Cadet.

The plane clattered its way over the Yorkshire moors as I went through my checks and eventually reached 4000 feet. I tried to make my voice as calm and musical as possible to make the

Cadet feel at ease; you could hear the voice all tight and rigid with concern at what we were about to do.

'Everything okay?'

'Yes sir'.

'Anything you'd like to do?'

'A loop sir'.

Always the loop. I had grown so used to the run of events.

'Okay then, my straps are secure – check yours are secure?' A short pause as the Cadet pulls the straps so tight they can hardly breathe.

'Yes sir'.

'Good, we have sufficient to recover by 3000 feet, cloud base is good, oil pressure and fuel checked, now for lookout I'm doing this slow right hand turn – I hear his breathing begin to quicken. "It's okay I'm not going to start yet, this is just the lookout turn to make sure no-one is nearby.

My instructor had done the same; a tight turn as I hung on in the back, thinking he had already started the loop and my reality began to disappear. It was like being on a roller coaster as it accelerates away and impossibly, you're left back where it started;

Even though your body is most definitely catapulting itself unstoppably forward – your head screams 'help' but eventually catches up.

'And here we go – full throttle – nose down' I eased the chippie out of the turn and pushed the throttle and stick forward; the engine picked up into a roar and the wind noise grew to a scream; we dived at the ground and the Cadet's breathing was now forcing itself through the mask like someone trying to blow up a balloon. I tried to offer calming explanations but I knew there was nothing I could really do, he was forcing himself through a rite of passage and I saluted him for it. There it was, something like 140 knots, the needle hovered over the gauge, the oil pressure wobbled about the usual place the altimeter was turning backwards round the clock 3500, 3300, 3100 – 'and pulling back on the stick – here we go – follow me through – pulling back – check the wings are level – now through your head back like me – look over your head' (the sky is now changing places with the green earth. On the wing tip I see out the corner of my eyes a simple circle of land rotating to become sky, my head is thrown back to spot the horizon as it slowly comes into view 'And here comes the land' We're upside down, momentarily, I love this moment, the wings are level, we're suspended 4000 feet over the North York Moors and I'm being paid for this...

I keep pulling on the stick and she continues the circle, ending up back in the dive again as we head towards a barrel roll, I know he's beginning to lose where we are.

'And that's a loop – into a barrel roll? A struggle whilst he tries to find his mask.

'Yes sir'.

'Okay I'm going to pick a cloud on my left – that one on the left wing-tip – see it? He answers with an increased pause, I know why. 'And we'll aim to turn the plane towards it whilst tuning her on her back – okay?' Ready?'

And off we go, rolling the red and white wings with a little rudder onto her back I end up pointing at the cloud, upside down, then pick another cloud out to my left and roll back round to face that – 'and that is the barrel roll'.

'Would you like to do anything else?' I ask rhetorically, letting the speed build up again and checking height as we dive towards 3300 feet.

'Stall turn sir?' Comes the reply, spoken as if he's clinging onto a rock face.

'Of course, and once again pull the nose up to point straight, vertically up and into the beautiful blue. If only we could freeze such moments, I'm working hard but know that this is the stuff that happiness is made of, and as I sit writing it I realise this is the moment when perhaps I begin to really enjoy it properly. For a moment the Chipmunk is flying vertically upwards to 4000 feet, I check the wingtips to make sure we're not toppling onto our back, the engine coughs, slows, I pull the throttle closed. We hang, for a moment, motionless, vertical. Two people, unknown to each other but for a radio mike, one behind the other, sat hanging above the earth.

I kick the rudder hard to the left, she slowly, grudgingly obliges and the aircraft pivots 180 degrees to change from pointing directly at the blue, to pointing directly at the ground. 'And there's a stall turn'. Silence. Yep, about now. 'You okay?' Silence.

I let the plane pull itself out of the dive and set the power to cruise her back to the airfield. I look back, the head is down, something is going on.

'Sick – sir'.

I know exactly how he feels. I couldn't practice aerobatics when my instructor tried to show me, something to do with the mind not being able to anticipate the movement. Every time we went up to practice spinning or anything involving turning upside down I would get out the sick bag, empty my innards and stagger back to the crew-room. I think my instructor actually began to feel sorry for me - and we were often flying three times a day. Once I was sick three times in one trip in a Harrier – the last time as we taxied in, the pilot up front giggling away at having made me a human vomit machine. I was poured out of the cockpit and rolled back to my bunk, but If you really can't cope they send you to the 'vomit comet' down in Farnborough – 'desensitisation' they call it, and spin you round and round in one of those funfair machines so that you don't know which way up you are, apparently you get used to it after six weeks of constant vomiting. Kill or cure.

I understood his predicament.

After a few minutes of straight and level he'd recovered somewhat, but the smell of warm sick was stinking out the cockpit a little. Had he hit the bag or not? Smelt like he hadn't. D'you fancy a go then?'

'Er, yes - sir'.

What everyone doesn't realise about flying is that it'll fly itself but for a few adjustments here and there. So often the Cadet grabs the stick and thinks they have to yank it about it keep it in the air, when all it needs is a light grip and small, subtle adjustments.

'You don't need to yank it about - here I have control – look – no hands!' I put my hands on the cockpit windshield to indicate no one is flying. But we're straight and level, we're flying, nothing is changing.

'You see – you don't need to do anything!'

To contradict myself I quickly radio back to the airfield and request permission to join the pattern amongst the usual commercial airliners, check the fuel state and oil pressure, look over my shoulder and bloody hell, there's Ernie on my wingtip. 'Hello – fancy a bit of formation?' He calls over the common frequency. Ernie was ex –fighters, an old hand and in his late fifties. He'd quietly snuck up on me whilst I waffling on and sat there bouncing around on my right wingtip a few feet away. I quickly put my hands on the control column and resume control, The Cadet was looking out in awe at the uncanny scene of another aircraft suddenly filling our giant, empty, agoraphobic sky and perching itself next to us as if defying some natural law. I took a breath and quietly scolded myself for my poor lookout and got the Cadet to wave as if this was a regular feature of my day.

After a few minutes the Cadet was following me through on the controls and I was letting them take her in a few 'S' turns towards the approaching runway; I just kept an eye on the gauges and height, kept an eye out for airliners and talked to Air traffic.

'There you go – you can fly an aircraft',

Teaching was that easy; the Cadet was happy, he'd done aerobatics, formation, straight and level and turning using the rudder and ailerons; what they didn't know was that I was thinking that I should be teaching for a living, full time, because I was getting a buzz out of showing someone another world.

I took over as we lined up on the runway, brought her down, closed the throttle and glided her onto all three wheels without bouncing... now just give me a Spitfire... taxiing her in wasn't easy either, you can only turn at slow speed by revving the engine and forcing air over the rudder, too much and the aircraft will 'ground loop'; that is, spin all the way round and you look an idiot. Plus the fact – don't forget - that you can't see a thing over the nose because it's stuck up at 45 degrees. Flying a tail-dragger is an art – on the ground.

I managed to taxi her in without hitting anything; the blue coveralled ground crew jumped onto the wing as I slid the canopy back with the panache of a Battle of Britain fighter hero – the Chipmunk had the ability to create that feeling.

Brakes on, chocks in.

'Got one more for you sir' He shouted over the staccato throbbing of the engine pistons chugging away in front. I wanted lunch. I was tired.

'Okay – strap them in'.

Another Cadet lurched up onto the wing, parachute hanging off them like a gorilla trailing its behind along, then lifted themselves in behind me.

Four in one day, this is hard work, I was sweating, hungry, I looked forward to... I stopped myself. Aerobatics. Four times in one day. One day I would remind myself that this is what I used to do, day in, day out. Who would believe me?

'Okay, what would you like to do?'

'Aerobatics please sir'.

It was a great few months of real work before I had to stop it all forever and head down to Finningley to start flying the 'Jetstream' - a twin engine turboprop where you read out the checks and worked in pairs. Gone were the days of punchy jet flying where you were the steely-eyed killer, gone were the aerobatics, gone was the freedom of the skies; from here on it was airways, transponders and flight plans, but I guess it would ready me for the world of civil aviation. I wasn't sure how I was going to cope with this.

Chapter 22

Playing chicken

So here we are, myself and my Co-pilot about to do something really stupid; why? Because I'm bored and have a chip on my shoulder about flying boring twin-engine trainers, so I dare him to a game of 'chicken' - both of us will walk to the back of the aircraft to see which of us will chicken out first and run back to grab the controls. No. We were not on autopilot.

We both unstrapped and checked the open airspace in front of us - the North York moors were far below and the weather was CAVOK - clear air and visibility okay. We looked at each other, ready?

We both got out of our seats with me giving the control yoke a final steadying nudge and keeping her as straight and level as possible... she was at about 9000 feet and with no turbulence - but then we both started walking away from the cockpit and down the passenger aisle. The aircraft was flying unmanned, uncontrolled, admittedly for a few seconds. As we walked back we got about ten feet down the fuselage before the aircraft began to rear its nose alarmingly; he ran forward to grab the controls whilst I managed to touch the back wall. I'd won.

Why do this? It was the sense that this world of flying had suddenly gone stale; that it was becoming tedious after the harem scarem world of fast jet flying; no longer buoyed along by our mutual sense of being fast jet jocks, something had disappeared - the attitude, the sense of dare - it was exactly like having not jumped from that balloon again and here I was in the also-rans - which isn't really true because I was a trainee pilot in a job most people would kill for.

But that's the problem with ambition in the RAF pilot world - most consider themselves failures of a sort; either they didn't make it to fast jets, or if they did make it to fast jets they didn't make it to single seat Harriers, or maybe they did make it to Harriers but they didn't make it to the Red Arrows. I guess the Red Arrows might just consider themselves successful. Maybe one of them really wanted to be in movies.

I look back on it as an act of insane stupidity; anything could have flown into us whilst we were down the back, we could have hit turbulence and found ourselves climbing the cabin floor to reach the controls. But in the moment I was just a spoilt ex-jet pilot who felt hard done by, who hadn't accepted that he was a mere mortal, and I guess I went some way to understanding how a 'star' feels when their false, temporary status is suddenly questioned and they too realise they're just human. My fellow co-pilot became a successful and well respected Captain on the Hercules - his reticence in walking away from the flight deck quicker than me was clearly a demonstration of his far more accurate sense of self-preservation - and awareness of air law.

Chapter 23

Albert

So as you can imagine, with a massive chip on my shoulder I arrive at RAF Lyneham just a few miles away from where I'd messed up last time at RAF Hulllavington - the home of II squadron. The constant mixed drone and whine of Allison Turbo-props hissed around the station, at times there'd be thirty to forty aircraft out there on the pan, but the first thing I noticed was that this was a twenty-four hour operation. No longer the familiar group of friends around the dining table, no longer the evening meal in a local restaurant, the crew room to hang out before and after flying to recount your tales of death-defying low level missions. No, this was a real job that meant flying with a crew for several days continuously and then pushing off back to your family afterwards.

It was the opposite of everything I thought flying stood for. The new Co-pilot is the butt of the joke for the crew as he's the youngest and newest arrived; you might find yourself surrounded by four other middle aged guys constantly eating pasties and sipping tea whilst setting the autopilot and checking in on the radio every half hour. I joined a trip down to Senegal; I found myself bored senseless whilst we just sat eating, following an airway and then eating again in the Novotel on the West African beach for a few days; the most exciting events were an attempted mugging and almost drowning in a canoe out at sea. But never mind the exotic beauty and real-life adventure, I was focused on food and I was used to eating whenever I saw food; but here was the first time I had to stop myself - because food was always available and always being offered and the smell of the hot oven heating up pies was always on the flight deck - it was like working in a kitchen.

I noticed other co-pilots had put on weight after their lean days as fast jet students, and it bothered me. It became a symbol for me of the loss of their status as jet jocks; the edgy fighter pilot would now lead a sedentary life sipping tea and eating cakes. I instinctively began to react, and if I only knew what repercussions would result...

So I began to run - a lot more than I had done in the past; my fear of getting fat was driving me. A psychiatrist had told me that if we feel like we've lost control of everything else in our lives, we turn to food and try to control that. It wasn't so much vanity as a need to prove to myself that I still had 'it'. I found a wholefood shop in Swindon, became vegetarian, adopted the Nathan Pritikin diet regime, and ran between 50-70 miles a week - sometimes twice a day. Sometimes I would eat very little on the flight deck because I wasn't getting a run in that day, sometimes I would arrive back in the UK at 3am local time, go to the mess, get changed and go for a run then - just to make sure I got that run in. I was becoming obsessive, but to the RAF this was impressive and initially I was applauded for doing the New York Marathon and getting the fastest time in the team with 2 hours 48 minutes. I went on a self-organised expedition and cycled the length of Mexico on my bike to discover the home of the very Tarahumaran Indians that Nathan Pritikin based his entire diet on. As I say, obsessive.

But I'd already failed the ground school. I was re-coursed to do it again. To a group of alpha males this was a no-no - an embarrassing inability to learn the basic facts and figures behind the Hercules; but it seemed like a wall to me; I was lacking motivation to fly this lumbering beast and dreaded the onset of four meals a day whilst being unable to run; nowadays, knowing what I do I would have just shouted at myself - 'just relax!' I'm just a thin person, we temporarily change in size anyway and this is a great job. Start drinking! But I became a non-drinking, vegetarian, obsessive running co-pilot. Man I must have a been a bundle of fun.

Because when you start denying yourself things, you start to crave them.

I began to binge eat, and like alcoholism it just creeps up on you. Problem is you can give up alcohol, you can't give up eating. I would deny for so long and then not be able to stop, followed by being sick, followed by instant hunger, followed by another binge. The two hour cycle, when it happened, was exhausting - and it was happening two-three times a week. What the hell had happened?

After some pretty lacklustre trips I found myself posted temporarily to RAF Marham to help organise an air display with a Wing Commander; it was then the Bulimia really kicked as I was being sick on a nightly basis in the toilets - this was reported to the Wingco and I was immediately told to report to a terrified station doctor; not only had I lost my squadron, but I was losing my flying category as they diagnosed me temporarily mentally unstable: A1 G1 Z1 became A1 G1 Z3. It was all going badly wrong as I was sent back to RAF Lyneham where they figured what the hell to do with me. If I binged I'd still try running in the evening - feeling like a beached whale - my weight changed markedly and I just couldn't control my eating urges. The Lyneham Psychiatrist would joke about eating his lunch after I'd explained how I couldn't consider eating just two sandwiches, it had to be none - or twenty five.

My flying cat' hung in the balance; I read plenty of books about Bulimia, I started to make myself eat three meals a day; I told the psychiatrist I was getting better, he signed me off 'fit'. He hadn't a clue. I was sent to a new ground school and a new squadron - 70 squadron - low level tactical flying - and dropping my old friends the paratroopers. Still running silly distances - but I was happier and understood my body and mind a little better.

So far I had not really made any friends, I was a little bit of an outcast but I was used to that; and yet this crowd were a likeable lot of highly successful aircrew who knew how to have a good time, some with a woman in every port, they were the modern day sailors travelling from continent to continent on a weekly basis. Sociable and usually drinking in the mess of a Friday from 4pm. And I was having none of it. I had no real friends and had lost my previous identity of keen, dedicated and committed trainee jet jocks; I'm all or nothing and it still worries me that there's no in between.

Onwards the real world of mid 1980s wages, miner's strikes and riots really didn't exist for us. Within our sealed little world of conservative values we just got on and operated the Herc'.

One day I came home and the phone rang... 'Pip here' came the reply - 'you and I are on the low level course together - we should hang out - got any tea?' I nipped out to get some milk and pushed open the door to find him at the top of the stairs to my flat -'hello - let myself in'. He dragged me out for a night on

142

the town in Bristol and it was like having a drink with Jim Carrey, Robin Williams and Anthony Perkins all at the same time - he looked like Perkins but could make you laugh like the other two. My social life took off as he recommended a date with someone really into aircraft; he just forgot to tell me she'd been married twice already; I'd not dated anyone in 9-10 years, so needless to say I was eaten alive and spat out. But Pip remained, and still is, one of the funniest and most charismatic people I've been lucky enough to meet on the way. He was also a natural pilot dammit, so his ease of RAF living was a model I was desperately trying to emulate and had to try so hard to achieve - and never did.

But amidst these years at Lyneham, the Hercules, Pip and a ridiculous training regime were some major adventures that need telling - and here they are... but before I do all that, just as I arrive on the squadron, it's time for me to mess up again/embark on the expedition of a lifetime (depending on how you look at it) and organise a month long cycle ride to Mexico...

Chapter 24

Crossing Mexico and finding the greatest runners on earth.

I'm arguing with the manager of a faded, peeling whitewashed hotel as he stands disinterestedly across the desk from me; why is he charging me for two nights? 'Dos noches senor'. After a hellish, fever-wracked night I cannot work out why I'm being charged double and my poor grasp of Mexican isn't helping ⸱ then my eyes fall on the newspaper on the counter in front of me - why does it say '23rd November'? Today is the 22nd. Then it slowly hits me. Today *is* the 23rd; there's been no time machine, no parallel universe. That really awful long night I've just spent in that room with the rusty fan, bare walls and bare tiled floors? It lasted forty two hours. I paid and staggered blinking out into the unforgiving white midday sunlight of Fresnillo's main square. I was unsteady, felt like I still had a very bad case of flu, and I had 70-80 miles still to cycle across the Mexican desert...

How did I get here?

As you probably guess by the title - this chapter has nothing to do with flying. In a way it's a reaction to being sent away from my beloved fast jet ambitions- which was just that - an ambition, irrespective of whether I enjoyed it or was good at it. But one thing I did love was to ride a bicycle - I hadn't learnt until late on - about nine or ten - but quickly made up for it. I was also a keen runner and was fascinated to hear of a tribe who could run races of 125 miles on a special diet; so I thought, why not go find them - by bicycle. So here goes the story of a one month, one man expedition to Mexico to find the greatest runners on earth and recover some self-esteem.

It all started with a book I'd been reading; since being sent to 'Fat Albert' and the Hercules from fast jet flying I'd become convinced I'd get fat, lose my edge, lose my drive, change as a human. That's the sort of thing we worry about when we're young, that our character isn't formed (maybe it isn't) so we, in our late twenties, think there's something, anything we can do before the rot sets in and we find ourselves in that rut of an armchair, a gut and a TV. So I picked up this book called the Pritikin diet - not a diet you understand - a way of living that has revolutionised Heart patient sufferers around the world with a low fat intake - yeah we've heard it all before but in the late eighties this was the beginning; nowadays all you have to do is google Nathan Pritikin to find out that he committed suicide at about this time after being diagnosed with Leukaemia, but that doesn't really throw out his philosophy with regards to a healthy diet.

The problem was that the diet was pretty extreme in terms of what you could eat, and I'm in the other extreme of an aircraft cockpit - no access to berries, smoothies, fat free steamed chicken or anything vaguely left wing and veggie. Pritikin based his diet on the Tarahumaran Indians of northern Mexico's Barranca Del Cobre or Copper Canyon. Naturally I had to find them - and by bicycle.

I discovered a fund in the RAF's stockpile of sponsoring adventurous types that was ready to back any nutter with a need to explore - The Trenchard Memorial Prize - and I applied for it. I wrote a plan, pitched my idea - they said well-done you've got it - here's the money and a month off - tell the air attaché in Mexico city and write us an article when you get back for the RAF News. Good luck. I'd just arrived on my first Hercules squadron and my boss welcomed this thrusting explorer who ran several miles most nights; within a few months he'd be cursing me...

I started in the streets of Mexico City, 6000 feet up and airless, hot and promptly headed out on the bicycle straight into the desert heat. I was warned about bandits, drugs, danger around every corner, but my main fear was rabid dogs dating back to my childhood; it terrified me more than anything, so why not pedal in open country with dogs roaming everywhere?

My aim was to cycle light, I had a tent that weighed two pounds made from Gore-Tex, a duvet jacket rolled around the tent, and a sleeping bag rolled up underneath the saddle. In the days before tablets I carried a two inch thick volume of 'Mexico on ten dollars a day', the rest was probably a pair of socks, two T-shirts, camera, passport, traveller's cheques and a puncture kit. One bonus was that you didn't need to book online like you do now; then you could just turn up at the door from the map in the book, knock and ask if there was any room. It usually worked.

The first stop was in a small village called 'Villa Del Carbon' after only about 36 miles; mainly due to the directions from passers by sending me the wrong way, probably due to my poor Spanish in the first place; hilltop, peeling whitewash and some sort of cobble street I seem to remember and a nice house *called* 'Posada Familiar; offering me a room for seven quid and a meal that started with a bowl of chilies - I thought I was supposed to eat them all out of politeness and did; the woman seemed surprised and brought another bowl - my head was on fire and I began to realise that it was just a side-dish...oh. I had hardly any stomach left for the beautifully simple main course of refried beans and enchiladas. It was perfect; a small village in Mexico, cycling and eating good food at last as the evening cooled and the shadows lengthened amongst the Yuccas, and all I had was my trusty Claude Butler bicycle sat in front of me - no petrol, no permit, no responsibility other than this wonderful blue machine.

But I check my diary and I'm staggered to realise that not only was I still going through my exercise routine *before* I started cycling! If I didn't cycle 60 odd miles I tried to run instead...this wasn't fitness it was mental obsession.

The next day I knock off 97 miles (hopefully no need of an evening circuit training routine) in the heat and the Mexican desert; but so caught up am I in my self-imposed schedule of fitness, routine, daily mileage and adhering to a plan that - though I set out on epics such as this - I am also slave to the schedule that got me here - and just like in the first chapter - I was forgetting to take in, be in the moment and enjoy what I was experiencing on the way.

I arrive in another small village with a few barren trees and a group of kids with their teacher playing the Piñata game where they hit the horse to get sweets out - now common place all over the UK and USA, but back in the 80s this was a lesser known Mexican custom and looked fairly exotic and interesting as I rode by; I stopped and immediately attracted the excited kids because I was white, on a bike in the middle of nowhere -

and it was about midday - where you needed sheltered transport. The young woman teacher was amazed I was from England: 'Please come to the class - we can talk to you and the kids would love to know all about England'. Let's just pause here; one of the prime reasons I wanted to go to Mexico - apart from the Tarahumaran quest - was my love of Mexican food from my trip to Belize a few years ago, and the stunningly beautiful Mexican women. So here I am, with my schedule... 'Sorry' I motioned in front of me to the attractive lady 'my schedule demands I cover a another sixty miles today...' she shrugged, politely understanding, and I disappeared into the desert, probably visible for the next five miles as a pinprick peddling furiously away from destiny. Pip has never let me forget that term when I told him that story 'must stick to the schedule...' and he's right. From that time on I've tried to live in the moment, and not get caught like that again. A pinprick I was.

Acambaro arrives and a 'Posada' - cheap room with no hot water or TV but about five quid for the night. Perfect. Like I want a TV or hot water in a desert? I'd pedalled by such outposts named 'El Oro' and 'Atlacomulco' where the twin towers of the Catholic church seemed ready to act out a scene with Clint Eastwood and Eli Wallach in 'The Good, The Bad , The Ugly' at any moment, all it needed was a lonesome whistling to Ennio Morricone's soundtrack. Dry, hot, and nothing but smiles and cheers from the passing Mexican motorists in their dust-covered wagons. I felt so truly in my element of exhausting, constant exercise that I just wasn't designed to stop.

There was no business, very little class difference, everyone seemed to work with the maize produce and that was it; you felt by being in the village square you were in the centre of things - no matter how small the village - at night it would come alive with eating and drinking crushed maize sticks rather than candyfloss, the girls sticking to themselves, the boys to themselves, and it was happy.

The next day I head to Salamanca, covering 60 miles and hitting smog and major highways where I am forced off by two lorries overtaking each other and leaving nowhere for me to escape. The wheels take a pounding on the roadside track I have to cycle on and I eat cactus leaves sold by the roadside; covered in dust I arrive in this industrial town where the white suited Police are pure theatre as they gesticulate and blow their whistles constantly whilst directing the traffic in the most dramatic manner possible - I begin to realise it's mostly for display as people watch and enjoy.

The early mornings are the worst - seemingly disinterested dogs suddenly spring into action as you pass them quietly on the bicycle - for them it's good sport and they gather in small packs to run after and snap at the hills. One near bite and my hypochondria will result in me cancelling the trip and running for the seven anti-rabies injections no matter how close they came.

By the next day I'm experiencing punctures as my spokes force themselves through the tape and start puncturing the inner tube from the inside; but I'm ready for this - I had this in my ruined summer holiday of 1980, suffering twenty one punctures in three days before I worked it out. This time I'm onto it - straight into a bike shop in Leon and a new strip of Wolber tube tape. Whether I have enough puncture glue is another thing - there's a lot of empty desert out there...

It's November 20th 1987 and my 26th birthday is spent cycling along the pock-marked roads, hooted and pushed off by the vehicles, at one stage stung by a small brown bee in my right chest; I immediately stop and pull my shirt off to see the insect fly away, his job done. It feels like a needle has stabbed me but I pedal on, eventually arriving in the twin towered town of Aguascalientes (mentioned in the comedy classic 'The Three Caballeros' where one expects the Magnificent Seven to stage a gunfight at any moment. My birthday meal is 'Frijoles con Tortillas y arroz' in a small café, and suddenly the food turns bad... bad soup, bad cheese, bad fried bread - what's going on? Have I stumbled on a town that just serves leftovers? I begin to think it's not the food - it's me. Things aren't tasting good any more, I really notice when I try to buy a tin of V8 vegetable juice while trying to watch Halloween III in the open air cinema in the beautifully cool town square at night - it's rank - and I'm feeling weak, taste gone, strength gone, very bad flu. I check into the hotel...

I pedal on to Zacatecas and then the little market town of Fresnillo over two days, covering 120 miles, suffering another puncture and going up a punishing slow incline and facing brutal headwinds whilst lorries just miss me and the surface gets worse. I find myself shouting abuse at this mixture of hellish conditions that doesn't quite fit my imagined picture of dusty Mexican desert roads. The hotel, 'Le Maya' has a broken window, bare floor and the local produce of Tacos, beans and rice is beginning to get monotonous. It's been a terrible night; I feel awful, feverish. Cut to the start of this chapter and me arguing with the hotel manager for what I think is one night's stay.

After what turns out to be *two* days later I stagger out onto the village square. The schedule, the schedule...without the pain of progression there is no rest, no enjoyment. Something needed to make me stop, and here it was. I blinked into the blinding midday sun and backed against the uneven wall of the Posada.

'Hey Mister - you don't look too good' came the voice of a passing villager. His name was Ivan Carrillos.

Ivan took me back to his modest flat across the street and introduced me to his wife and small child; they told me to stay there while he got a doctor. I have no idea how much time passed, it might have been weeks but my diary says just two days. I remember their pet Collie dog putting his snout over the end of the bed and just watching me with a look of genuine concern in his eyes; it began to hit me how ill I was as the doctor came and weighed me, no one spoke English but we all tried to understand each other, nevertheless the doctor seemed puzzled. He wanted to know anything I'd eaten, drunk, been bitten by anything? I remembered the bee - I pointed to my chest and made the internationally recognised buzzing impersonation. He examined and was convinced. Killer Bees he motioned and explained in broken English - they reach Aguascalientes. I had been stung by a killer bee. I thought it was a bit strange to have such flu in Mexico. Ivan and Ylena looked after me for another night and by then I was desperate about 'my schedule', but as the evening approached an old 1960s pick up turned up with several Mexicans wearing upturned sombreros clearly with the aim of taking me and Ivan for a night on the town.

I found myself amongst several Sombreros clinging to the cab of open top truck amidst many cheering lads in big hats as the word 'Cerveza' was repeated and a bottle was thrust into my hand; man I would love to spend a night on the town with a bunch of exuberant, friendly Mexican geezers who clearly knew how to hang one on - but the day after I've recovered from a killer bee attack? It didn't help that was pretty well a teetotal 26 year old who knew little of the world. I look at my younger self with mild frustration - the least I could have done was to drink myself to oblivion and stagger home amidst cheers. Having said that, that's pretty well what I did - I remember the dark town square lined with those small fairy lights, I remember many dark Mexican bars and being introduced and standing out as the only white dude for miles, lots of Sombreros and then another Cerveza, back in the truck - hang on - pull up - another bar. Kind of like a night out with a Herc' crew but with a shorter distance between bars.

Next morning Ivan gave me a gift of a Bible and a note wishing me luck. I was blown away by their sincere kindness, but for me it summed up the attitude of Mexico - everyone I met across the length of the country was trusting and helpful; the night out and instant friendship from strangers, their acceptance of me - even though I could hardly drink; Ivan and Ylena's complete care for a stranger and the cheer of the locals towards me in the darkest and dingiest of bars impressed me no end. I can only hope to show the same hospitality should some newcomer to my country be suffering in a similar way. I'm not good at it, I suffer the same suspicions and mistrust as the next bigot, but it inspires me to try harder. I cycled away from Fresnillo much richer.

I set off north once again and wish I didn't have an expedition grant that required I explore the home of the Tarahumarans; I

152

was knackered and recovering from bee attacks and far worse - Mexican drinking nights with the locals and I wasn't feeling very much like exploring the origins of hyper-fit endurance athletes. But my obsession and focus on the schedule kept me cycling onwards and upwards towards Chihuahua.

Every now and then I had to contact the British Embassy and try to talk to an English Captain who was tasked with my welfare should I run into difficulty; it was always a problem, trying to talk to the Mexican operator and then usually getting his wife to pass a message on to him when I did get through. One time after a lengthy conversational difficulty with the Mexican female operator I was offered Spanish lessons (from her) if I was going to stay in the country for a little while... even more incredible is that I think she was genuine, it wasn't a come on. As for the Captain, he must have thought of me as some kind of lunatic who was probably going to be heading for the North pole after this, and I might have, had my career not suffered as a result. Because you can't go back to the UK and carry on eating Arroz Y Frijoles. Oh, and cycling 70-80 miles a day.

It's just one long straight road after another as I stumble between the potholes and cause the passing trucks to hoot. I'm spending about £12 a day on accommodation and food, living off Tacos, raisins and corn flakes during the day and night stopping Torreon (109 miles), Bermillo and Ceballos, sometimes a couple would wander into my room (double booked), sometimes I'd get a hot shower and TV, sometimes someone offers to fill my water bottle, offers of lifts with the bike in the back of numerous trucks - I smile and wave them on, idiot I was. But it was like that all the time.

I'm now practically living on cornflakes and raisins as a staple amidst the Frijoles and Arroz and not paying much more than £10 a day for everything. Unbelievable. A truck driver runs out from the isolated desert side café, stops me to ask whether I'm a professional 7/11 team rider... and it's about time I saw a bandit; but nothing, just friendly, easy going people. The town of Delicias wins the biscuit though; not only am I asked if I'm okay by passing motorcyclist, I'm then offered a room by a family running a stall, stopped by car asking if I want any help, finally a local girl (Liza Bukti) helps me by offering to translate in a local bank to change money - can you imagine that happening in the UK? Then again, what kind of hopeless vibe was I sending out?

But it's now early December and I'm feeling very tired; I've covered about a thousand miles since Mexico City and the effects of the bee sting are still present as I arrive in Chihuahua, I've got chest pains and the mistaken choice of hot chili sauce gives me hiccups causing pain in my lungs, it hurts if I break into a run to cross the road. Nevertheless I'm still knocking off 60-80 miles a day out of Chihuahua and in a few days I'll reach my eventual goal and home of the Tarahumarans - the little village of Creel deep in the Barranca del Cobre (The Copper Canyon). But until then I'm resting for a day and coping with something I never get - headaches. What is happening to me? The final 80 miles to Creel is looking like a wall... the food is mostly against all my ideals - fry ups with eggs, cheese, and my hunger from all this cycling always seem to result in me over eating on the very stuff I came here to avoid. I'm also not really thinking of the future as I follow this idyllic existence as if I was a professional cyclist who is going to train every day like this for the rest of my life. What was I going to do when I got back? How was I going to live and eat and not train at this level every day?

After being sent the wrong way by three different sources I discover there is still 90 miles to go to Creel and give up - jump on a train - bike travels separately and arrives four hours later. The maps are that bad that I need to rely on my bad Mexican and a dodgy map of a little known area of the world; So I'm out, consider myself a wimp despite having covered over a thousand miles, arrive in Creel by rail and find a place to stay for about £4. It's still not the real thing - this is a village - the settlement where the Tarahumarans live is 8km away in Atacacas, but Suddenly, I see a Tarahumaran in the street - an Aztec style cut with a weathered face, white loin cloth around the midriff and walking barefooted, clearly no wish to adopt the ways of the villagers.

So I'm cycling the next day to Atacacas along rocky roads, 9000 feet up and suddenly people are living in caves hewn into bizarre rock formations and yet the everyday washing is hanging up outside. Nothing romantic, nothing picturesque, just people living in caves. I guess the rent is minimal and bills are pretty low.

But for some reason I needed to go deep into the canyon and use my ultralight tent, otherwise why the heck have I carried it and my sleeping bag, on my bike, for the length of Mexico? After somehow enlisting the services of a guide and interpreter, I watch the Tarahumarans partaking of a dance that had been going on for the past three to four days - non-stop - I also managed to wander about their caves and note everything they were eating, largely consisting of Corn, Pinto beans and Tortillas, but with the odd discarded bottle of Sprite and Coke, and even a slab of cooking fat; I'm not sure whether they choose to live like this or feel they have no alternative, because there is a railway into Creel and the local town has plenty of westernised Mexicans who clearly live the average 'western' lifestyle. I felt I needed to get out there in the wilderness and see the country these people grew up in.

It seemed like a mistake. Cycling down a road that gets rougher and rougher until it was just rocks and descends further and further into a canyon, the sides of which can be higher than the Empire State building. Every now and then I see a short, ten inch stretch of tyre tread, then nothing, then a bit more, then nothing. It is only when I see a Tarahumaran with his guitar (usually a violin) and wife and realise he's wearing sections of tyre tied to his feet that the mystery s explained - and he's crossing the road at right angles as if the hilly, barren wasteland surrounding is the real place to be walking. I come across two kids I presume are on their way to school - and the last small group of wooden houses that might house a school being at least ten miles away; clearly growing up here is hardy.

But there's no movement in the little collection of wooden shacks that is the nearest thing to civilisation on this rubble track that I'm now having to walk the whole time. A man chops wood, the dogs have shut up and don't care about me wandering by. The Tarahumarans seem fully aware of an easier way of living - a pale bloke pushing a bicycle is clearly no big deal - but just get on steadily with their way of living. The barren beauty and loneliness of this giant valley is akin to a Sunday walk to the gliding club in Portmoak - a permanent Sunday seems to be going on and I decide that I'm not going to

156

hang around here. Just see it, live amongst it and get out; I began to crave civilisation.

Which is why setting up a tent for the night in a deserted canyon probably felt so alien and forbidding. I was homesick for food, TV, roads, people, sound, the proximity of something. Because for thirty odd miles I'd seen less and less of anything, let alone shacks where you could purchase food, water; in theory it always sounds wonderful - just pedal until you hit nightfall and then lay under the stars in the Copper Canyon...

I was terrified of bears. Maybe one would smell me a mile off and seek me out, crushing my tent with one paw and ripping me to shreds at 2am in complete darkness whilst I try to run. I remembered the film 'Alien' and the tagline - 'In Space, no one can hear you scream...' well, clever me, I'd found the equivalent in deepest Mexico and arrived with nothing but a single skin Gore-Tex tent. The place was called 'Humira' on the map and arrived as the sun was lengthening the orange shadows; it consisted of three wooden shacks at the side of the rubble, long deserted. I saw a stream meandering further down and decided this was the least barren of campsites with a little bit of green to shelter amongst (from what?). It was weird, similar to a feeling I'd had as an eleven year old on a trip to the New Forest; then I'd felt particularly vulnerable to the elements - a thunderstorm or - something would destroy *everything* we knew - until I realised the car was reliable and offered protection. But here the fear wasn't inexplicable, it was due to there being nothing between me and the elements but a thin sheet of Gore-Tex, bleached bare canyon sides and positively no one about mad enough to be here at this time of night. Apart from (quotes excerpt from the Mexico guide book as he props bicycle by the tent) 'Bears, Jaguars and Coyotes...'

I stay outside, surveying the area for wild animals and reasons to move on until eventually the light fades pretty fast and there's nothing left to do except get inside my man-made coffin. It doesn't help that the tent is in fact coffin shaped and very small, and green, all the more chance of a wild animal stumbling over me and attacking in fright or fear. I lay still, petrified. I hear a heavy footfall no more than a hundred yards away - what could make that sound? It would have to be big and heavy. If I was outside right now would I be looking at a magnificent spotted Jaguar wandering past? Should I just jump out the tent and leg it now? Crash. There it goes again...

I remember deciding that I just had to go for a pee, and crawled out into the night to look around at the scariest scene - scarier than any predictable carnage in a horror film - to be utterly alone and yet staring at loose bush and sparse vegetation, an otherwise pleasant river running past, knowing that anything that emerges from it is going to be focusing very much on you, makes you feel like a definite target - you feel watched and probably are *being* watched - and they can outrun you.

Next day I awake to freezing cold - a frost and the water in the bottle is frozen as the shadow of the morning moves slowly down the side of the canyon - you could see it crawl down the towering steeples quite majestically - and all just for me and the watching bear. In the meantime before the sun hit I had to get going or suffer frostbite - it felt that bad and that cold. When the shadow finally crossed the river bed it was like turning a heater on - bang - daylight is here and so is the heat. After ten miles of uphill rubble and walking the bike I finally hit tarmac, passing a gathering of Tarahumarans thousands of feet below gathered round a campfire on a hilltop - I guess that's where all the people were heading yesterday. Meeting? Festival? I have no idea, let's face it I found out very little ; just a tourist observer passing through to take photos... and although I would go on to jeopardise my entire flying career with my attempt to continue this diet as some kind of attempt to continue this active life, I did knock off a 2:42 marathon in Berlin and a 2:48 in New York a couple of years later, having followed this regime and been a right pain in the neck back at the Lyneham Officer's Mess. So maybe I did take something away with me from this experience after all.

I spent a week living in and out of Creel, taking cigars (what?) as payment on the advice of a local guide, whilst being allowed to nosey about their caves and see what they're eating and doing as if I'm latter day Doctor Livingstone; but I just felt like some rich gap year traveller who's read a book - which wasn't far off the truth. I was treated with distracted politeness at all times - as if there was something far more important to do than show me about, but if I really wanted to - go ahead. I didn't need the cigars either.

The cinema in the town was the only entertainment that was from the outside world, I remember walking to the old stone building, the film was 'Legend' with Tim Curry; I settled down for 90 minutes of escapism even in this harsh environment. Suddenly the projectionist disappeared behind the screen and a noisy generator clattered into action, he gunned it to full revs and left it at that - full blast whilst the film then started - I couldn't hear it over the generator; the audience didn't mind because they were reading the subtitles... I just sat there and watched the slightly blurred image of Mr Curry act out some incomprehensible set of events, and I've never watched it since. A chance to keep the unblemished memory of Creel perhaps, those cool nights in the Indian town with the sense of discovery on the edge of western influence. One day I'll watch it and relive - but I can only do it once.

Funny how my diary makes no mention of an excellent American couple I remembered spending some time with; nowadays this is the sort of the thing I would record - human contact. Not food eaten, distance cycled and money spent - pointless - but that's age and experience I guess. I think they were both part time models - he for GQ - which makes them sound of a sort - but anything less like the stereotype. Chatty, engaging and genuinely interested in my relentless cycle ride, I'm not sure they believed me when related my marathon training, the distance I'd ridden, the fact that I 'd planned and been sponsored on my own expedition, and then to cap it all, they asked me what I did that enabled me to do all this... I think that's where they stopped believing me. I have a way of apologetically explaining things I've done because I can hear exactly how it must sound even before I actually say it. So it comes out all sheepish, as if I'm slightly ashamed; 'Erm...Pilot actually, no really, kinda worked my way up I guess - you know - from the ranks, I run the odd marathon, well quite a few - all under three hours - I've just cycled about - oh - a thousand miles from Mexico city - no really - to find the heart of the Tarahumarans and kinda study how they can help me to run faster and longer.   All in one evening over blue tortillas, arroz y frijoles. Eventually they went a little quiet when they asked about my job ('is this guy just spinning one yarn after another? - look at him - he's just doesn't look the type') but to me they were a lovely couple, and are up there with Ivan and Elena back in Fresnillo as one of the many decent, considerate types I had the chance to spend time with. I didn't meet such people in my blinkered career, and I felt that the only way to have such experiences was to make these fantastic journeys of near physical exhaustion - as if these hidden people needed to be hunted, needed to be earned. Nowadays I think I have a clearer idea what I'm after, human contact, but without the necessity for physical punishment on the way.

I got around to asking the guide about the epic runs of the Tarahumarans - known as 'Rarajipiri' and they were having one in a few days where they kick a ball in front of them sometimes for 120 miles (so the rumour goes) but this one was 15k. Looking back, I should have asked to join in, but one had the feeling it was a private affair for the Tarahumarans; all sorts of rituals were followed - smearing the legs with oil and goat grease, boiled cedar branches, watched over by four old men who are not allowed to sleep, they only eat food prepared by relatives such as rabbit, deer and Turkeys; all this is to guard against cheating - which is apparently a regular occurrence (which you might think would explain the incredible distances - but this is too commonly an acknowledged fact). Most of my diary documents obsessively the food I ate, the money I spent (about £1.50 for a big meal) and the research I made into the Tarahumarans for my research expedition article I was expected to write.

The chilly evenings were spent in a restaurant, sometimes by candlelight due to the frequent power cuts, and wondering what everyone dos in the evening; the cinema was usually empty, and there was even a disco, which I really wish I had tried - for the experience alone.

On the 15th Dec I guiltily catch a coach back to Chihuahua (why the guilt? Because it feels like I'm still forming; what I do now will influence the rest of my life) ride with aching toe, numb hands and one front light to the Aero puerto, fly back to Mexico city and spend an evening talking to the owner of the only Vegetarian restaurant in the city about the home of the Masons and the greatest mason of all apparently - Winston Churchill. I was treated as if I came from the Promised Land and he seemed surprised that I didn't revere and respect this ancient, secret order.

I spent the rest of my time wandering Mexico city and looking for souvenirs, of which there were surprisingly few; it wasn't a tourist spot really; what looks like thirteen year old kids stand on street corners with shabby uniforms and automatic weapons bigger than they are - guarding the bank and looking as if the street gangs have taken over. I'd cycled a thousand miles, I'd camped once, though I would have liked to do more but for the diversion brought on by the bee sting. Back then I regretted the delay and change in schedule, nowadays I would welcome it with open arms, embrace it, hang out with Ivan and his mates in Fresnillo, hang out with the Americans in Creel, give a talk at that school I passed by, maybe I'd have found a way to talk to those Tarahumarans properly; then again, maybe I wouldn't even have left the shores of the UK, which I don't very often these days.

I expected to do more, says I at 52 in 2014 looking back on 1987. I'd started with the Netherlands, crossed the Alps in winter, pedalled from Sardinia, Corsica and up to Paris, now I'd taken on the length of Mexico; next was supposed to be the `Sahara, but it just didn't seem a practical possibility, and now I never seem to have the time or money - and the Sahara in the current political climate isn't a good idea. Unfinished business perhaps, or the ability whenever I get on a bike to know I've taken these wonderful contraptions across continents.

The conclusion to my diary reads like this...

'Catching trains for last stretch due to wrong turning, worrying about time (obviously knackered as well) also regrettable. So I don't feel totally elated; but it's the longest and most 'outback' ride I've completed yet, so an achievement is made. My chest still hurts badly, pulse has been very high throughout (normally 44-48) has been 57-62. At moment in Mexico City 87! Is it the altitude?'

I went on to return and run some of the fastest marathons of my life before drifting into Bulimia and nearly losing my flying category; for that reason I was considered a victim of diets and because the career suffered, it was a bad move, but in terms of what to eat, attitudes to consistent training and experience of an entirely different attitude to life, I'd witnessed something. I also try to be like Ivan when a stranger wonders into my midst - but I'm not as good as him.

I may not have crossed the Sahara by pedal power, but I like to think I now meet people without thinking of schedules, and can probably write a whole lot better now - I guess that's real progress.

Chapter 25

In which I end up owing my life to a fellow crew member

The Herc' was fighting its way through the snowstorm, ice on the wings, a dim light shining from the cockpit and five men peering nervously out of the windows.

A Norwegian accent erupts out of the static:

'When established on the glide-path clear descend for ILS approach'.

Bardufoss – a treacherous Norwegian airfield in the middle of its winter. Mountains stand sentinel either side of the runway and this means we have to fly a very accurate, narrow approach path down the middle of a ruthless no prisoners ravine to reach the runway; the only problem is that the snowstorm had obscured the airstrip and we're having to fly through the middle of a whiteout, purely using gauges that do nothing more than indicate navigation beacons which we fly towards.

We enter the fluffy cloud-tops at 7000 feet - now blind and descending amongst jagged peaks that we couldn't see but we knew were below us, then next to us - then above us. I was staring at what looked like a fuzzy TV set, with no ejector seats, no parachutes, and no powerful engines to climb out and escape with. I believed in the instruments in front of me, what a strange, sudden trust I had to adopt - my life to needles and mile numbers that count down on the meter in front. The friendly Norwegian voice in his warm, safe tower calmly brought us the bad news:

'Be advised the cloud-base is registering 200 feet.'

We have to see the runway lights by 200 feet or we have to overshoot – that's the rule.

The Captain is focused on the dials in front of him, one hand on throttle levers and other hand on the battered 1960s control column - we're still descending, now passing 3000 feet. The navigator sits just behind me, monitoring the approach on the radar, reading out the height we are and the height we should be passing; the flight engineer sits between myself and the captain, looking up at the fuel and monitoring us; we're a team, all backing each other up in our suddenly dark world of red lights, flickering needles, engine noise and blank TV screens that were once the windows, caught in the this invisible valley of certain death - if we get it wrong.

'Enough fuel to divert to Alta, skipper... 'says the Engineer.

'Cheers' mutters the Captain - as his eyes flick from gauge to gauge.

We're in a dimly lit cockpit with orange lights flickering figures at us; the stifling smell of recently cooked pies wafts through the heavily laden air, the sound of the four turbo-props constantly whines through our earphones.

I switch to tower frequency and call for landing clearance.

'Ascot 251 you are clear to land...' (there comes a pause from the tower that says 'you ain't gonna' make it') 'be advised runway visibility currently 80 feet in freezing fog'.

'We'll give it two tries', mutters the Captain over the intercom – 'if not we'll overshoot and head for Alta - Eng' keep an eye on our diversion fuel.'

I try to focus on the Captain flying the approach accurately, which involves his keeping two needles in a crosshairs and by adjusting the aircraft up or down, left or right, depending on what the needles are telling him, at the same time I look for the dull glow of the runway lights – if he loses it I might have to take over, but we have faith in the instruments, faith in science.

We're approaching our decision height – the needle slowly shows us getting nearer and nearer to the ground and we can't see anything – the only thing that tells us we're just 200 feet above the ground is the dial in front of us; outside is the same bland windowpane of a whiteout, but there are mountainsides hiding, lurking, ready to reduce us to a blackened smudge on the ground. I scan whilst he focuses on the height and speed. Engineer is also peering over my shoulder, Nav' checks his dials.

'See anything?' 'Nope'. 'Overshooting – full power – follow me through.' I tell Tower we're overshooting. Tower: 'Call when established on the missed approach procedure.'

A perfectly reasonable request - but this is where it all went wrong.

I start reading out the headings and heights for the Captain to fly: 'Fly straight ahead to flight level 30 (that means setting a new a standard pressure setting on the altimeter of 1013 millibars which will make all aircraft altimeters read the same height over 3000 feet).

Captain: 'Okay setting standard'

We wind our altimeters to read the new pressure setting of 1013.

'Approaching flight level 30'. It means our altimeters will be in synchronisation with other aircraft cruising the airways, but inaccurate in terms of our actual height above ground. Yep, you can see what came next ...

It was beginning to get busy; we're in a whiteout flying very close to mountains trying to turn in a big circle and start another attempt at the runway - it meant accurately flying on instruments, relying on the navigator for plotting our position, the engineer for monitoring our fuel and balancing, the Co for talking to ATC, the Captain for flying the heights within at least plus or minus fifty feet.

'Okay at five miles on the TACAN readout; make your heading 170 degrees. I'm map-reading for the Captain, all he's checking is his artificial horizon, his altimeter and his compass in his selective radial scan as his horizon shows thirty degrees of right bank, his compass slowly winds itself onto 170, the speed remains at 150 knots, and the bank is slowly taken off as the Hercules settles on 170 degrees.

'170 degrees' comes the Captain.

'That checks' comes the Nav' to back me up.

We fly downwind, then turn again when abeam the runway – between us are mountains but the Nav' confirms we're clear to turn – and so does the map in front of me – eight miles from the TACAN beacon on the runway – time to turn onto runway heading of 010 degrees.   Once again the Captain pulls the control column down to the right to show thirty degrees right turn on the horizon - before levelling again as the Hercules drifts itself round past the big 'N' of North as he begins to level out to show 010 degrees, height and speed remain constant - that's good flying.

It's beginning to get really dark in here – the cloud becomes dark grey as we approach the descent point:

'Nine miles'

'Beginning descent... now – flaps to twenty'

I move the lever and watch the flap gauge slowly move to twenty degrees – this means we can fly slower without stalling.

'Pre- landing checks' calls the Captain.

The Nav' checks them off one by one:

'Gear?'

The Captain nods - 'down'.

I pull the lever and the trundling sound of hydraulics that confirms the gear's moving – five seconds of rumbling and the three green lights confirm that it's down.

'Gear down.'

Hydraulics – 'checked'

Booster pressure – 'checked'

Flaps – 'twenty'.

'Checks complete.'

I pull the switch on the column without interfering with the controls 'Ascot 251, checks complete, confirm clear to land.'

'Roger that Ascot 251... You are clear to land – advise visibility now 100 feet.

We descend – into darker and darker grey – perhaps we're nowhere near the airfield and are about to crash into random Norwegian mountains - but the sense of flying into a deep ravine is now very strong. I know these crew members as fellow drinkers in a bar, nothing more, perhaps a pint on a Cyprus hill, perhaps a meal in the mess, that's all; and yet here we all arè in a very intimate situation, a life threatening moment where we must all be very trustworthy, discover our faith in gauges, our faith in each other, our ability to remain stable when nature's ultimate power surrounds us and out-climbs us. Ignore all external feelings – fly the numbers and watch the gauges – that TACAN beacon mileage readout is your lifeblood. That altimeter height readout is your distance above death. That altimeter...

1000 feet - passing five miles.

Suddenly the Navigator interrupts:

'Hang on - stop – we're still on 1013.

I look at my setting with sudden disbelief - the small numbers in the window of my altimeter confirm which millibar setting we have on the altimeters and mine says 1013 - it shouldn't. We should have changed it to the local airfield pressure setting or our altimeters will over-read; which means read higher than we actually are, which means we're in danger. Just how low are we?

'Roger that – full power' says the Captain - no pause, no check - instinctive reaction. It may have saved our lives.

Immediately I push the levers forward with one hand on them and the other hand quickly winding my altimeter pressure setting dial to d=find out our real height above Bardufoss runway – the height needle spins down to –

'Call radar tell them we're diverting to Alta'

'Roger that'.

We climb, the cloud becomes brighter, and the Engineer confirms we've enough fuel for our diversion of Alta. Eventually we break fluffy white cloud again and settle down, level out. The crew take a quiet deep breath.

How far had we gone with the wrong setting?

200 feet? 100 feet'? 50 feet?

We all wound our altimeter dials down to 982 mb - but already the power was on and we were climbing – we went from an indicated, incorrect 1000 feet to a correct, accurate *370* feet in just a few seconds. We had been about to hit the ground and it wasn't a runway – it was the mountains a few miles in front of the runway and it wouldn't have been a landing - it would have been a fireball.

We diverted to Alta and said no more about it, but we'd all learnt something today as we played that over and over again in our minds; how had an experienced crew forgotten - en masse - to reset the altimeter from 1013 mb to the local airfield setting as we started our descent to the runway? Busy, workload, four crew members miss it. The Navigator probably saved our lives - thank you Ady.

Chapter 26

Peeing in the cockpit.

I bought an aircraft. Here it was in front of me. £6500 amounted to a small contraption of wood and canvas painted blue with a red stripe down the fuselage, an open cockpit, no radio and a Volkswagen Beetle engine for propulsion.

My first flight would be my first solo in this machine – it was a taildragger – which meant it was tricky to land. The disused runway on the edge of Huddersfield was surrounded by high ground and a few gravel pits I didn't want to end up in – if I had an engine failure on take-off (I used to own a VW - broke down every other trip. My mate also had one and we had to abandon it due to blue smoke suddenly emerging from the dashboard). I was a bit cautious.

I taxi out in front of the eccentric owner – he's dressed as the Red baron watching, complete with goggles and leather flying hat. I give a wave and shove the meccano-designed mechanism forward, the engine responds with the roar of a? Well, a VW – and we – no 'I' am suddenly trusting my life to canvas, wood, a few wires and a 1960s car engine. In what seemed a moment of irresponsibility, I gingerly pulled back on the stick and somehow rose into the air. Suddenly I was at home. She flew. The wings waggled when I moved the stick, the engine kept clattering and the micky -mouse altimeter indicated two hundred feet. Okay so far; let's try a little bank, bit of rudder. Yep, she's turning just like a real aircraft. A very slow, real aircraft.

I'm flying on my own, the wind is on my face and this is about to be mine – mine to fly when and where I want. Richard Bach, Antoine de Saint Exupery here I come. Patagonia? The Sahara? Ernest Hemingway? Was there no limit to my expeditions and the literary exploits I would embark on?

I brought her back to land quite gently, closed the throttle and taxied her in. I guess the owner trusted me since he knew I was RAF and hopefully somewhat trustworthy. He stood there in his full length leather coat as if to debrief my strafing run over the British trenches in a Fokker Eindecker:

'Great – yep – it's a deal'. Is there a toilet and a phone anywhere? I needed to spend four hours in this cockpit and sort out how Lyneham would clear me to land.

We shook hands and I handed over the cash like some second-hand car sale. I had borrowed a hand-held radio (wedged in my flying jacket) and knew there would be no toilet stops on the way – finding an airfield and landing without a radio might be considered somewhat rude; I had written down a list of frequencies on the way but that was no guarantee with this radio. I also wanted to stay clear of controlled airspace since I had no navigation aids to follow and would therefore be incredibly illegal.

It was going to be the old way. Map, compass and a bit of luck.

As I took off and slowly climbed to about 500 feet I found myself almost enjoying the undulating greenery of Yorkshire, until I realised it was one of those chilly October days and I needed the toilet again. That might be a problem. Never mind, press on.

I also noticed the compass was pretty well useless, the moment you touched the rudder off it went spinning like a demented top. One thing for it, fly straight and level, let the compass settle, pick a point on the horizon and fly to it. Seemed to work pretty well. I glided over the fountain of Chatsworth House and flew the length of their beautiful stately garden – this was flying. But I must keep an eye out for Alton Towers as that's a no fly zone – should be well off to my right.

Hello? What's that? Ferris wheel and some corkscrew metal – right below? That'll be Alton Towers then. Bugger. Right over the top. I turned her away and sent the compass spinning again. I was way off my intended track which meant I needed to alter heading – but I was now dying to go to toilet.

It was like one of those dreams – or horror stories - when you really want to go to toilet and you imagine several different scenarios of how you will actually go – in the wardrobe (no), in the alleyway (what alleyway?) In the sink (of course). But here there was no option. I couldn't land because there was no airfield nearby and this bloody radio wasn't in range of anything right now. I knew how I'd do it; loosen my straps, stand up in the cockpit and go over the side – if I could keep the stick steady between my legs I reckon I could get away with it. I actually started to get up and then thought... what the bloody hell am I doing? What did I think this was? Something out of Those Magnificent Men?

By now I was bursting and where the hell was I? I could see the faint towers of a major city. Lots of towers. Birmingham? Bloody hell there's a ten mile control zone around that – right now I was probably some unidentified blip that they were re-routing airliners around. I had a brainwave. Go to toilet sitting down. In the cockpit. Just go. What does it matter? It's your aircraft Laurie. Not really my way of assigning territory, some would put a name on the side; me? Far more radical; just piss on it. Or in it.

Ever tried peeing yourself? It's hard. You have to make yourself do it. But once you start, it's very hard to stop. And then ten minutes later when a slight urge comes again and you're sat in a damp cockpit you just have to carry on – and I carried on for a good few hours that way. My new aircraft. It soon became an incontinence bath-tub of hell.

I avoided Birmingham by giving it a wide berth – I ignored my spinning jenny of a compass and just looked for something I could recognize; eventually I found the M5 heading south. At last I could gain my bearings and sort out the route; it was then that parachutes appeared in front of me. Not that far in front. Quarter of a mile. How pretty. How dangerous. A few more. Look down, light aircraft, windsock. Airfield. Parachute zone. I yank the stick right and avoid the no-go danger zone as best as possible. Well at least I know exactly where I am. I note the parachute zone on my map – outlined in red.

There was nothing left to infringe. If I actually had a licence when I landed I would get a decent compass fitted in this jalopy and pay the various fines. I followed the M5 until I found the left turn with the M4 which would point me at Lyneham and home. You ask me how could I expect to land at a busy RAF airfield without a radio? Aha! – Along with everything else that had been planned for. That was the reason for my phone call. They were expecting me. How could it fail? It was simply a matter of telling them my ETA and when I pitched up I would circle a few times above the runway and they just had to fire a green flare to clear me to land. That was the plan.

Strange. No flare. I circled. A Hercules transport taxied up the runway waiting to take-off. Ah that'll be why. Then I see the smoke trail of a flare, but what colour was it? Couldn't see the colour, just the smoke. Hmm. Better keep circling. Five minutes pass. Hercules still waiting to take off below. He fired another. Just caught it – green. Right.

I was about to set myself up downwind to land when I realised the windsock was pointing the wrong way – the wind was blowing from the east and the Herc' was going to take off with the wind – how strange. But I had to land into the wind so spent another five minutes trundling downwind to land on the eastward facing runway – pointing at the Herc' – that crew must by now be cursing me in there cockpit.

I put myself on finals and lowered the nose at the same time easing the throttle back – immediately the engine cut out. The prop flicked itself to a standstill. The VW clatter was no more. I was 500 feet up and suddenly a glider.

I pushed the stick further forward to keep her flying – luckily the runway was already beneath me and she settled onto all three wheels with the quiet trundle of a shopping trolley. There I was, sat in a urine soaked open cockpit homebuild in the middle of a major runway with a Hercules and its four engines burning away waiting to take off. I unstrapped, stepped awkwardly (and damply) out of the canvas and ran round to the back. Picked up the plane with my hands and proceeded to wheelbarrow the plane off the runway like a naughty child who'd strayed onto a main road. As the Herc' roared past I thought of an apologetic wave but it didn't seem interested.

The tower had sent some airman in a land rover to pick me up. It wasn't quite like Allcock and Brown crossing the Atlantic, or Charlie Lindbergh arriving in Paris having flown the Atlantic solo, it wasn't even like Bleriot crash-landing in Kent having just made it across the channel. This was 1987, everything had been done and I'd managed to make it epic by sheer bad luck, a dodgy compass and probably a hefty dose of bravado mixed with incompetence.

Needless to say, the airman was desperately trying to stifle a giggle. I looked a bloody idiot in leather flying hat, goggles and a toy plane that had just stopped working. I hope he hadn't spotted the damp leg, or the smell as I got in the passenger seat. We tied the naughty child to the vehicle and towed it back to the hangar.

But it wasn't over.

Outside the hangar I put some chocks in front of the wheels and decided to give it an engine run to see if I could find out why it had stalled. I set the throttle at idle and span the prop. Nothing. Spin again, nothing. Perhaps a little more throttle? Spin again – it roars into life – full throttled life. Oh dear. At full power the aircraft begins to lift its tail (lucky the chocks were in). It goes on lifting. For a moment I consider running at the cockpit to pull the throttle back but luckily remember there's a prop at full power spinning in front of me. Over she went onto her nose. The prop splintered into a thousand pieces. Immediate silence.

Someone laughed.

Techies came out of hangars and offices – everyone laughed.

I looked around, unable to blend in and disappear since I was wearing the aforesaid heroic aviator (clown) uniform. Adopted sheepish, painful smile. At least no one had died. But the day was still young.

A Sergeant airframes and engines expert offered his services and later that week he'd checked over the engine and declared it airworthy once I'd stuck a new prop on it.

But stowing it in the hangar wasn't easy either.

One morning in the Officer's mess I went to put my toast in the four-lane multi toaster and there was some leftover pieces left wilting in the toasting bays; clearly forgotten. I removed these pieces and planted my own. Suddenly a Squadron Leader wandered and casually threw my virgin pieces to the side and replaced with his dank and forgotten pieces. I shrugged and ignored him; petty idiot. I thought.

Needless to say my interview was with the Officer Commanding Engineering concerning asking for hangar space to store the plane. As I was ushered through the various glass-panelled corridors in the back of hangar empire of the engineering world

I was eventually shown to the office of … I saluted the toast thrower…

'Good heavens you've got no chance' was his immediate reaction.

'Very sorry about the toast sir'.

He was actually quite decent after all, he allowed me to keep it free of charge in some well-kept hangar. But the incident shook me; I suddenly had to be nice to everyone on this base. I couldn't be the cavalier aircrew thinking I ruled Lyneham any more. Keeping an aircraft meant responsibility dammit. But most of all, it meant realising that you were just a small cog in this world of aviation and you needed to be nice to Sergeants and Commanding Officers alike. Most importantly, you needed to be nice to engineers.

I considered this run of events to be more than just bad luck. Something told me that there were some pretty tragic outcomes that could have resulted from the many things that went wrong on this day, in fact I'd been pretty lucky.

I sold her two years later.

Put a deposit on a flat.

Which went into negative equity.

Chapter 27

Night fighters over the Ivory Coast

I'm on the way to Africa with a couple of crews aboard 'Fat Albert', the aim was to learn how fly into pleasant and exotic countries like pre-revolution Liberia and The Ivory Coast - which would come in handy when the Westside Boys kicked off a few years later in Sierra Leone. But never mind the flying, the night was the real learning curve.

I stumbled into the crew party room of our white washed, wooden town centre hotel in Abidjan; the Ground Engineer or 'GE' had already mentioned the 'night fighters' and all I could see was the back of a rather large woman staring at a semi-circle of nervous RAF crew members as she told them the order in which she would 'see' them; I quickly worked out what the term 'night fighter' meant and edged back out the door, they all looked sadly consigned to their doom – such was the authority of this woman's voice.

That was our night stop in The Ivory Coast.

The next day it's Liberia and we're crammed into a yellow taxi, one of the crew is standing on the roof as we bounce down the dried mud main track to a village known as 'Smell No Taste'; I didn't believe it either, in fact I thought I'd been duped by the locals for the last thirty odd years until I googled it just now – and there it is. The man pretending to surf on the roof is one of our Captains and at any moment we're probably about to lose him.

So we arrive in town just as another taxi passes us with the rest of our crew – they're shaking their heads – danger – turn around they seem to say and point the other way; naturally being in the dense bush miles from anywhere with a pre-revolution state about to be toppled, we ignore them and plough on into the village. What could the problem be?

We turn the corner and find ourselves surrounded on both sides by curious Liberian youths, who, to any uneducated white types growing up in the Home Counties in the 70s, would assume dangerous. They quickly gathered, sitting and leaning over a few iron railings on both sides of the road that finished abruptly in a dead end. We had a choice, do what the other car did or fake complete 'at ease' and try to mingle. 'Hello'...?

We offer to the local, intense faces of a remote village that probably don't get two car loads of cheering, high-spirited white blokes appearing very often. A moment passes. I say again, pre-revolution Liberia, there are apparently a lot of angry people about and we're about an hour north of Monrovia and I don't see any Police stations around here. They come closer, a hand is extended...

To say we met with politeness and intelligent, intensely interested conversation would be an understatement; the youths all wanted to know about education opportunities in the UK, many had ambitions like any educated person you meet in the UK of 17 or 18, but here, most couldn't see how this would happen; their spirit was nevertheless undaunted. I'd never experienced this before; educated, intelligent, forthright human beings are, usually in the UK, clearly on their way to University if they can afford it and a reasonable career. Here, in this tiny village there was exactly the same level of thought and interest in the outside world, aims to be aeronautical engineers and the like, but how were they going to escape this place? It is only recently that I realise that these youths of fifteen, perhaps seventeen, considered themselves grown men; unlike our teenagers who needn't grow up until 21, 22, this lot have been out earning since they could lend a hand to their father; these weren't your teenage rebels but in fact responsible adults who knew the benefit of an education. It was then I discovered the reason for the name of the town; apparently there used to be an American base a few miles away and you could smell the cooking drifting over the bush, but could never taste it. On closer inspection and questioning there appeared to be a local recording studio, but for now we were invited to enjoy the nightlife – the local disco;

A Portakabin. This was their Saturday night entertainment – one Infra-red light on the far wall and music coming from some tinny speaker underneath; as a keen Michael Jackson fan I was genuinely dancing with our self-appointed guide to the tune 'Liberian Girl', which wasn't quite true to the emotions of the song as she was about 40 and our friendly, unofficial guide for the night; nevertheless I remember the purple light, the almost empty hut, people kicking about outside. It was by far the most unlikely disco I'd ever come across.

Unfortunately there were a lot of taxi 'scams' on the trip; the crew would claim an extra taxi and spend the extra money on beer. And yet it was the Co-Pilot's duty to look after the funds; not surprisingly usually the youngest and most easily coerced member of the crew, wishing to remain popular and in league with the rest, he tended to go along with whatever was hatched. No surprise when someone told me we had run out of cash; as the Co-Pilot, I had to phone up our man in Monrovia, ask for some Air Attaché about an hour's drive south and tell him the news; apparently we needed to pay for the 'fuel' – and he kindly drove all the way up the rough track with the spare currency. It's hard to disagree when an entire crew is deciding for you – and you're not the Captain, but I don't think our man in Monrovia would be very happy to know that it was in fact, paying for beer. On arrival back in the UK I refused to sign this off, said it was illegal and I still remember the look of silence from the two Captains, who promptly got some other Co to forge a receipt. You can imagine how many crews wanted to fly with me after that. But I'm told things are very different now.

After several hours flying to make an approach into Timbuktu – not surprisingly in the middle of nowhere - I note a single fire truck and a hangar – and we chose the only time of day when another aircraft is coming into land on the opposite runway. Of all the times to try and approach into the most deserted and inactive runway in the world we chose to be head on with another aircraft on finals – and were instructed to overshoot. We were short on fuel and that was it – off to Algiers.

Like I say this was another trip but let me explain the Co-Pilot's dilemma; I was running about Algiers airport trying to find out about passport control and flight plan clearance when suddenly a particular Captain getting rather flustered, shouted at the top of his voice for me to stay where I was, right in the middle of the airport concourse; It's tricky because as a Co-Pilot you're expected to somehow find out and use your initiative in these unknown airports, but at the same time you're supposed to be at the beck and call of your Captain; I was being told the former and was trying to make my point, but you can try too hard.

That evening we were treated to an evening out with the Algiers Air Attaché (no cash required this time) and presented with our very own bills at the end of it; bear in mind Coca Cola was round about ten pound a pint in the late 1980s. But the stuffed dates were superb.

My experience of Senegal was a night in Dakar, it was my first trip in a Hercules and staying in the Novotel on the coast, we arrive at the airport and park on a sun scorched bay where the grass and weeds spring between the cracks and surround the plane with bush like some old 1920s painting of the first air route across Africa; I feel like Sir Alan Cobham. A man in overalls connects the fuel pipe and needs dollars – cash. I pay about two thousand and hope it goes to the right place as an off white van pulls up to take us to town, as we all get in with our bags and kit and large black lady runs over to us carrying several bags of oranges and asks with a thick cockney accent if she can hitch a ride with us, all the oranges spill out and we're amidst tumbling oranges with a native Londoner who we assumed was a local about to try and sell us her wares.

The Novotel was where the rich tourists hung out, where a walk on to the beach would result in a man grabbing your wrist and trying to escort you to his mobile beach front shack of cheap trinkets, then a glance at hotel security with his stick and the grip would loosen; I had never felt the iron grip of two fingers to be quite so powerful, but I forced him off me and caught a taxi into the town.

Dakar's streets were dry and the street lamps were slung on ropes between poles – the lamps would sway amidst the night mist and the light breeze blowing onshore; I walked into a thatched, half lit restaurant and ordered the finest swordfish and groundnut sauce, whilst further down the street the crew stayed safe in the Irish bar, eating pies and swigging bloody Guinness.

But the next day I ignored their warnings about Dakar and caught a taxi into the centre; the driver was Indian and insisted he waited for me where he dropped me, I felt another scam coming on and ignored his nods and affirmations that he would be right here when I get back. So off I strode in my bright new multi coloured shirt into the marketplace looking like a rich American tourist in his mid-twenties...

Not long after I was befriended by a tall athletic man in sunglasses and flip flops who wanted to show me pictures of his family, give me small trinkets and show me round the market, what could be the harm in that? I let him follow and found it rather awkward to refuse his constant gifts and barrage of talk about family and the locale, it was then he started asking me for a gift, a token of my respect...

Nowadays I would probably have assented and agreed, for the sake of hospitality and the fact that I might be reading him wrong, but in my mid-twenties I was outraged. I see your game I thought to myself...

'You give me the money or I give you the knife'.

Ah. Bugger.

I looked around, two legless kids crawled across the road on wheeled trollies – this was a harsh forgiving place and it was like one of those films where our hero suddenly realises he's in the wrong town, the cue ball hovers over the pocket, the juke box stops working and the barman ducks behind the counter.

I keep walking.

'You give me the money or I give you the knife'.

'Oh that's not right I thought you were telling me you were my friend and now suddenly you come out with this what kind of message is that to an overseas visitor?'

I still couldn't see the knife. He towered over me, all loose shirt and flip flops, the disabled kids on homemade trollies sat and watched. I made a dash for it, where, where? The next corner? This corner? I wasn't sure whether he was after me but he looked like he would have much trouble, a very white guy in a very loud shirt running through an African town, great. I turn the corner...

And there he was, my greatest friend in all the world, the Indian taxi driver grinning from ear to ear with the engine running as I leap in and slam the door shouting 'drive' and throwing dollars at him all in one movement. He was off.

'You were right'

'Ah yes' he grinned.

So they were my African experiences, perhaps naïve, mostly painful where the crew were concerned, but very rewarding where the locals were concerned. I met consideration at every turning as well as prophetic foresight from the taxi driver – and

I'd go back just to taste that thick groundnut sauce once again, I felt privileged to have glimpsed the mythical Timbuktu and enjoyed my dinner with the Air attaché in Algiers; but most of all I remember the lads in Smell No Taste, the sense of denied ambition that showed no bitterness or resignation, but remained polite, interested in the world and provided a real quality of conversation you'd be hard pressed to find anywhere in central London.

Just writing this makes me want to go back there.

Chapter 28

Arrows pointing at Kuwait

I'm cycling up L'Alpe Duez - that's the famous winding road that the Tour De France does every year at breakneck speed despite the 1 in 5 slope that practically makes it impossible to stay upright on the bike. So when I get to the top I'm knackered, ready to kip, before working my way through the rest of France. I check the TV on the wall in the local bar. My French isn't very good but the TV says it all; there's a picture of Saddam Hussein and lots of arrows pointing from Iraq into Kuwait. This looks like something should be interested in, in fact I should probably phone my base just t check what's going on.

'Hello Lyneham? 70 Squadron please - it's Flight Lieutenant Tallack... quick transfer to the Squadron Leader... 'Where the fuck are you?' I'd filled in a leave pass; 'France - the Alps'...'What? Came the reply when mobile phones weren't widely available. 'Get back here ASAP'. 'I'm on my bicycle' 'Stick it on a train, get straight back here'. And with that my French tour of the Alps was over - all because I'd checked the TV on the bar wall.

I was back in about 48 hours and tasked to fly immediately - ferrying kit to Cyprus (ten hours), followed by refuel and fourteen hours off, followed by ten hours to the Kuwaiti border, refuel, turn round take off and another ten hours back to Cyprus, 14 hours off in the RAF base at Akrotiri, followed by another ten hours back to the UK; fourteen hours off, then start all over again. Quite a schedule, and we kept this up, most of the time, for six months prior to the start of the land/air war. I did 75 visits to Cyprus, It's still a bit too soon to see the place again, and it's been at least 22 years. It's probably the hardest I've ever worked in my life; in the midst of this was one attempted relationship with the woman who loved aircraft - eaten alive - and the ongoing bulimia causing me to eat entire pots of Halva and packs of hobnobs when under stress; everyone else just smoked incessantly on the flight deck or drank heavily right up until a few hours before take-off.   We carried 9mm Brownings, humped aircrew biological warfare clothing everywhere we went and generally sweated continuously whilst sharing a few non-air-conditioned rooms with five crew in one of the Akrotiri huts with one of those fans that spun and whirred like the fan in 'Apocalypse Now', interspersed with this would be my pathetic attempts to use a payphone to contact my one month relationship or check my answerphone to see if there were any messages from her - invariably there wasn't.

I realise that if you don't get married a relationship isn't seen as 'serious' by many people; but I think Oscar Wilde put it accurately when he said that 'one may bear the absence of old friends with equanimity, but even a momentary separation from someone whom one has just met is almost unbearable'. My 'relationship' was one month, and it hit me like a divorce. The sense of pointlessness that I felt, having covered many thousands of miles to the Kuwaiti border and back with many stories to tell, hoping for that flashing light on the answerphone when I got home, the sense of hope and expectation was a massive driving force - equated only by the sense of utter despair to see the steady light on the phone - indicating 'no messages'. No messages after a week of expectation and imagination as to what you might tell her.   I truly began to feel that I was not cut out to have a relationship whilst I was travelling like this continually; it made me desperate, in need of female company, in need of reassurance. It wasn't healthy, and it had been ten years.

Here's a few of those stories from an actual war which I thought was for the right reasons.

Chapter 29

Gulf War 1: Transporting the 'Ooligans'.

'Are Special Forces being sent to the Gulf?' read the Captain as we sat, seemingly motionless 27,000 feet above the Saudi Arabian Desert; we were flying eastwards on a Sunday afternoon, looking down on a curiously pink landscape.   I looked over his shoulder at the Times Editorial. 'On the ball as ever' came my reply.

We'd been going back and forwards to these rapidly forming airfields for nigh on a month, but the war hadn't started, Saddam Hussein was enjoying his new found possession of Kuwait and all leave was cancelled. As I wandered down the back into the cargo bay for a pee the volume of noise increased from the cockpit cacophony to that of a large machine factory in full flow, I clambered amongst the tied down equipment, tightly pulled cargo nets and hooks embedded into the floor; normally clambering over recumbent passengers with ear defenders; some asleep, some gazing into nothing, some reading. There'd be inevitable questions like 'how long?' shouted between their eating packed lunches and having miss-calculated how long they'd be stuck without amusement in the chilly, partially pressurised hold of a Hercules.

But this time there was a difference; unlike the usual passengers, these guys knew how to travel via Herc'. No using the uncomfortable red nylon para-seats for them; oh no, they strung up hammocks from the roof like a flock of bats bedding down for the night, slumped in their own privately customised beds pace swinging idly from the ceiling - wiry, quiet, self composed individuals; from us they needed nothing.

I reach the ramp at the back of the aircraft, pull back the plastic curtain and am faced with the time-honoured urinal; an interesting contraption resembling a waste paper bin, such as you see nailed to lamp-posts in the street, but at waist level. You pee into it (if male, otherwise you've got the chemical toilet) and hear it sucked away into the slipstream, probably landing on some unfortunate far below as a fine mist of rain, best they don't know. I peer from behind the curtain because the equipment that I'm standing between and clambering over consists of armoured outboard engines that wouldn't look out of place on a competition class power-boat, deflated raiding craft, curious weapons, trussed up, bundled like some regular delivery of toilet rolls.   I take a closer look through the cargo netting at one of the outboards, complete with armoured cover. This is not the usual bunch of government-issue rifles either, exotic equipment is to be found between the grey, worn, criss-cross tangle of the cargo nets, all covered in the ever-present chipped and worn colour of green. A small war could be fought from this cargo bay such was the firepower, but right now it all looked about as innocuous as the urinal I'd just used.

For a moment I ponder the surrealism of this half-lit, droning hall of inactivity, brimming with potential chaos, disorder, efficiency beyond the realm of normal human capacity. Here before me are the athletic Marine elite; lying inert, dozing, waiting in limbo for their moment. But right now this might be a village hall for all its sense of menace. I feel like some sort of privileged onlooker and then note one of the fellows has pushed down one edge of his hammock with his finger to have a look at what I'm up to. Dam, even now, ever alert. I nod, smile, move on.

I climb back into the cockpit, connect up the microphone; 'They've got some good kit back there'.

'The hooligans are in the one behind us' came the Captain.

As I looked out over the Captain's shoulders I read the Times editorial as it conjectured and wondered; for once we in the military were, to be precise, 4000 miles ahead of the Press.

Who knows what they'd be up to or what awaited our cargo; we were still months away from conflict and Saddam was threatening blue murder. I didn't envy them, but I took one last glance at this little team of placidly slumbering individuals as they rocked back and forth in their hammocks, and allowed myself a smirk of being for once 'in the know'.

Chapter 30

'It'll just be a routine check...'

After two weeks of solid flying backward and forward to the Kuwaiti border they spotted that the crew was in need of rest, that we had flown more than anyone else, that our Captain was going through a messy divorce and saying 'yes' to anything that came his way. I don't blame him, but we'd had it and finally someone noticed; our checks were of date, our flying categories needed updating; so, half asleep I was immediately thrown into the cockpit with a flight checker and told to fly to Exeter and do an approach.

'It's okay - said my Captain - it'll be a formality' - just to re-validate my 'Green' status as competent pilot on instrument approaches. I'm wasn't so sure, but they wanted it out the way, done quickly. The 'Can do' spirit. I'd done it before and proved my competence.

But I was tired, half asleep. I drop below the minimum descent height by thirty feet. Fail. Quite right. But what wasn't right was taking that test. I'm downgraded to 'amber' rating. I regain it a few months later, but it was a critical time;

'Can I just have a word Laurie' - I was called into the flight commander's office - 'shut the door'. Oh dear. 'You're due to be posted to Riyadh for the crew detachment, but in light of your recent problem with the flying categorisation, we don't think it's in the best interests for you to go - I'm sure you understand.'

I'd nodded and saluted and walked out, closed the door. Then felt pretty unworthy. The whole nature of this job is that you all pull together and suffer the same risks, the same experiences. Scud missiles were haphazardly being chucked at Riyadh on a nightly basis and the resident Herc' crews out there were coming back with all the war stories from their six week detachment - mine was coming up. It wasn't bad luck, I'd messed up at a critical moment. It may sound strange now to want to be under fire, but I wanted and expected to be sent there - It was a fundamental part of my job. Pip had volunteered, but I just expected to go anyway and awaited my turn. I felt somewhat short changed here. I was beginning to wonder about the chances of my making Captaincy.

Chapter 31

Duelling binos'

So I'm flying the leg down to Bahrain again for about the tenth time in a month; the Captain has been whining on about the bargain binoculars he got at the duty free, 20x magnification and only £50; but the flight engineer has a got a similar model, only cheaper (yawn), how long we got to go? I figure it's the right time to quietly pull out my Russian telescope bought recently for a tenner with 50x magnification and peruse the desert below.

'Where'd you get that?'

'Dixons' in Chippenham

Silence.

Having achieved temporary purchase superiority I inform them all I'm off for a pee. Clamber out of my seat, take off the headset and head down the back. But hell hath no fury like a scorned Hercules crew with nothing to do for ten hours - when you're off the crew microphone there's no telling what they'll cook up between themselves.

I arrive back and slide into the characteristically familiar dried sweat canvas of the Co-pilot's seat.   Hello, I think to myself; that landing light has been left on. I felt sure I switched that off as I raised the gear on take-off. Hmm. Oh well, I'll just wait till no one's looking and switch it off; the crew seem pretty quiet -

Flight engineer's reading a newspaper, Captain's checking radio frequencies, Navigator fiddling about with his charts. Lean across, flick the switch down, there. No problem.

Captain?

Yes what is it Loadie'?

Captain, there appears to have been a burn out on one of the landing lights back here in the hold.

Right - what might cause that?

Engineer - 'usually if a landing light has been left on when the gear is retracted'.

Oh shit, I'm thinking - can I get away with this?

Captain: Well - let's check the landing lamp panel - nope - they're all off so can't be that.

Engineer - yeah - I noticed - that's really puzzling - that's the first thing I checked - they've definitely all been turned off. Must be something else - might be serious - might need to divert.

Loadie - Well it's burnt out the undercarriage housing - quite serious. You sure it's not that?

Engineer - yeah you absolutely sure Co?

Oh well, best own up.

Me: Well - okay - yeah I just turned one off - but I'm sure I'd turned it off on take-off.

Captain: Ah!

Engineer: Oh dear.

Loadie: I knew it.

Me: What?

Engineer - Oh dear - that's a flight incident report - needs to be filled out - wasn't the boss talking about this the other day?

Captain: Yes he was - it's an incident report situation - you'll need to fill out a form 1001 right away - so you can fax it immediately when you get down. I've got one here.

Me: I honestly didn't think it was that serious.

Captain - oh it's very serious.

Engineer - I think it's an automatic Squadron Commander's interview

Navigator: - Depends if it's a first offence...

Me: First offence?

Silence, they'd gone too far. You Bastards I'm not falling for that. The lamp has an auto cut off if left on. Not bad, they'd had me going for a few minutes - but not long enough to make it an anecdote - and they knew it.

Back to the hum of the aircraft; clearly it had been worth a try, but they'd have to work harder than that to catch me out. I picked up my telescope to once again establish my ocular viewing superiority. The eye piece felt slippery.

Engineer - here's your lunch box Co.

I turn round to grab it - why the interest in my face? Place box down by side and resume the telescope - hello - what's this? The greasy eye piece has been coated with boot polish.

You bunch of kids.

No one would admit to it. The landing light circuit breaker is pulled and the engineer flicks the switch on to make it look like the lights have been left on.   When the Co goes to turn them off the whole crew play the game that the Co has messed up. Usually works, just a question of how long they can keep it going.

Well, it kills half an hour, nine and a half to go...

Chapter 32

Autopilot problems

Imagine the scene on one of the many trips to Cyprus; the aircraft is in a gentle descent, outside is the Mediterranean, inside the Captain is attacking the flight deck with a mallet. Yes, a mallet. Why?

I wasn't on this trip, but the Captain and Co-pilot are well drilled in knowing the seven different methods of disengaging the autopilot in an emergency; you can turn it off, you can push the controls hard, you can even press the little red 'autopilot disengage' button, or you can do any one of the written down methods we've all had to learn (and I've forgotten); point is, there was *no way* you'd ever *not* be able to disconnect the autopilot if you really had to. Unless you'd found an ingenious method of getting round all seven of Lockheed's failsafe thirty years in service C-130 Hercules' flight systems...

Yeah we did.

So this crew were coming back from one of many Akrotiri trips during the first Gulf War, but earlier on the autopilot switch had broken in two pieces; which meant the two pilots had to spend nine hours actually flying the aircraft - which is quite hard work (which is why we have the autopilot). But hey presto! The flight engineer has a brainwave, he disappears with the two halves of the circular switch, and the Captain continues flying, his muscles aching, holding the height and considering diverting.

A little bit of technical info';

The autopilot is engaged by settling the aircraft in whatever attitude you want - descending. Climbing, straight and level, then lifting the circular switch upwards to pull up a central knob - thus engaging the autopilot. The aircraft will now maintain the climb or the descent or straight and level. Not like fancy airlines that will land the darn plane and taxi the thing into the dock for you, pretty straightforward really. Lesson over.

The flight engineer comes back with the circular switch in one piece. 'Well done' they all say as he places the switch back over the autopilot knob and thus renders it fully workable again. The autopilot is clicked in just as they're cleared to descend from something like 25,000 feet to a much lower height - something like 7,000 feet - this could be have been for weather, diversion, but I don't remember.

As they approach 8,000 feet the Captain presses the autopilot disconnect switch to being the levelling out that'll settle the aircraft at 7,000 feet. He presses. Nothing. 'Co, try your switch'. Nothing. He resorts to disconnecting at the circular de-tent button. He can't move it. It's stuck. All seven methods of disengaging are tried with no result. The aircraft is in a steady descent that cannot be altered and 7000 feet is fast approaching as the altimeter winds itself towards the number seven. The Navigator reads out the emergency procedure from the cards, still nothing, pull, kick, the autopilot will not disconnect. The aircraft is in the next events must have taken place at the speed of light:

The Flight Engineer sheepishly offers an explanation. He used quick drying glue hold the switch together. The glue appears to have hardened. The autopilot is now glued into the 'on' position without any means of disengaging it, in a descent and fast encroaching the airspace of other much faster moving airliners. Captain flashes a look of disbelief, normally it would be funny. Lockheed missed that one.

7000 feet wanders past.

Captain shouts for something heavy - like a Mallet. Mallet appears from loadmaster's stores (they've got everything) Captain attacks autopilot with Mallet. Button goes down. Autopilot disengages. Captain pulls aircraft into level flight. Everyone breathes out. I guess they flew it home manually.

Chapter 33

Pouring me out of a cockpit...

Not content with cycling across Mexico, spending all my time training for marathons and buying a light aircraft, it's not really surprising that something had to give. My time on 30 and 70 Squadron had been a lot of work but I wasn't getting recommended for Captaincy and I faced a two year ground tour on a Simulator - total failure in other words. So where do you send someone who's failed Captaincy? That's right, to the most ambitious, capable and 'gung ho' bunch of single seat fast jet pilots in the business - to a Harrier Squadron at RAF Wittering.

It wasn't so bad. To be honest I was left pretty much alone to 'fly' the 14 million pound video game on a daily basis - to test out the carrier landing facility, introduce visiting dignitaries and practise air to air refuelling. I sat Harrier pilots in the seat and ran them through emergency drills, and I guess I got pretty good at 'flying' and operating it. Then 'N', one of the pilots assigned to the Sim', invited me to go along on a 'recce' in a real Harrier... (Photo-reconnaissance training flight)

'Yeah sure - can we go via a mate's house?'

'If you like - give me a grid reference on an OS map we'll get a photo...'

'It's down near Bath - can we do that?'

'It's on the way'.

As we swaggered out to the two seat 'T' bird, one of the techies asked if he could also have a photo of his house just outside Peterborough:

'You sure? What if there's an unknown car parked in the drive?'

'I know all about the milkman.'

Strap in, mask up, canopy closed, familiar smell of rubber everywhere, sound of raspy deep breathing through the headphones. Last time he'd taken me up I'd been sick straightaway, he loved making multi-engine rejects like me suffer.

Now let me pause here to explain something; I always got a rather confused stare from instructors when I came back from instructor-led aerobatic lessons having had to stop the trip due to acute motion sickness. Motion sickness can be quite simply your brain not predicting movement - so when you're driving you don't get sick - but as a passenger you do. The same goes for a jet - I can fly a jet through plenty of tail chases and aerobatics, but stick me behind someone as a passenger and it won't be long before you're likening me to Mister Creosote.

'N' spun the finger to signal start, waved the chocks away and we were off.

It was akin to sitting astride an express train that has been neatly compacted and squashed into the space under your seat and between your legs - you feel like you're astride a rocket that could easily get out of hand. But it doesn't feel like Science fiction; what with the old dials, chipped paintwork and worn rubber grip on the control column, it feels more like a late 1950s madcap Jules Vern invention that you've just discovered and might work, might not...

'I'm ready for you this time 'N'; I shouted down the intercom as he taxied out'. Bad idea.

He let out a knowing laugh.

'Right watch this'.

As this bloody great beast of a rocket, the finest piece of engineering Rolls Royce had ever invented was about to demonstrate one of the most wonderful take offs known to man - as the power lever went forward and the Pegasus kicked in, my head shot back in to the ejector seat, someone punched me hard in the spine and I was suddenly left about thirty feet behind, like I was sat on the back of a motorbike with an imbecile in command and had fallen off the pillion with the acceleration - but was still being dragged along by my hair - as 'N' calmly commentated the facts of our science:

'Here goes the nozzles...'

And with that the whirring, clanking contraption of turn levers and buckles leapt into the air like nothing I'd ever been near in my life, and suddenly the world is moving past us in a smooth procession of fields, pylons, roads, housing estates, then ooooomph...

'Just taking her left mate'

He caught me out but I'm already forcing the blood back into my head and tensing the stomach muscles. He won't catch me out that easy. We settle for skimming the treetops to his first photo opportunity.

'There she is - just to the left of the pylon'.

Somehow he's found the techies' house just to the west of Peterborough. We sail past with the house 45 degrees to our left.

'Got it.'

Wham - I'm sideways again and fighting to breathe as sweat bursts out of my helmet and 'N' sets course for Bath. I realise that my G suit has failed full 'on' - it grips me like an iron glove - legs, stomach. I tell 'N'. He laughs and his head goes down as the throttle goes forward. In ten minutes of tree skimming we're approaching Lyneham - my old airbase.

'What's the frequency for Lyneham?'

It's ten miles away, but that makes it thirty seconds away to having to call them. I know the frequency by heart.

'Lyneham this is Harrier XV 1789 for low level run and break departing to the south thirty seconds request join'

'Roger XV 1789 you are clear'

'I'm gonna bomb your old base mate'

Once again I see his bone dome go down as he literally rides the machine like a motorbike as he hurtles like a hooligan down runway 07 then breaks left and sets course for the local village I pointed out on a map just half an hour ago, I note the heater has also failed full on.

'My heater is blowing full hot'

Another maniac's laugh from the front seat as my head is yanked to the left, I look sideways at passing roads, cows and trees before I'm thrown up right and apparently 30 seconds away from Whitley. Pylons, houses, fields...

'There she is - on time - on target'

Where? - Bloody hell -

'Back there'

'You sure?'

The world turns sideways and sweat is now flowing quite happily out of my head and down my face as we turn 180 and skid across the Wiltshire countryside like some joyriders in a stolen Porsche. Apparently we're getting paid and apparently this is legal.

The iron fist is still gripping my stomach, the heater is still full on and is getting the better of me and I'm sick into my bag like a pro - I've done it enough times. How 'N' becomes aware I have no idea - but he's onto it.

'You honked?'

How'd he know? Maybe if I admit it he'll take it easier heading back...

'Yes'

'Hahaa!' that means he probably won't.

Like it was some kind of challenge. As we sped back with gut wrenching twists and turns I managed another full offload of anything I'd eaten in the last ten years that might have hung around, kind of like a reverse colonic. I filled two bags. Surely no more. I was wrong.

A we landed I was akin to a wet blanket that had been through a wringer, I was ready to be poured out of the cockpit. Yet no, such was 'N's incredibly aggressive taxiing ability - with such sharp jabs of the brake he should consider bus driving as a secondary career option - I managed to vomit for a third time as we taxied in. Needless to say 'N' thought it hilarious - three times!

I staggered away from the aircraft and somehow made it to my room in the mess, fell onto the bed face down and then suffered diarrhoea for the rest of the night and the next day. It was like recovering from flu and a heavy night out at the same time. The problem is that you immediately become branded not only as someone who cannot take 'G', but someone clearly incapable of operating such machinery; when in fact a few years ago I was the one pulling G, popping aeros and hitting things on time, but stick that me in the back seat and I'm suddenly 'the passenger' and the body and mind seem to accept it all too readily. I tell that to my friends today - who frankly don't think me capable of rewiring a plug let alone landing safely in a thirty knot crosswind. Then again, that new wiring system on plugs today is tricky.

The pictures were reproduced within the hour and he'd hit everything bang on, no computer, just compass and stopwatch and a 500 mile per hour beast. Some people you just have to watch, suffer the piss take and admire the skill. Cheers 'N'. Hope you got the Cathay job and hope you're not too bored.

Chapter 34

Christmas dinner like no other...

We're all dressed in Mess kit - cavalry style trousers and ridiculously silly blue waiter style uniforms, and it is at such times you realise that the RAF is run by a lad's club who will jump at any excuse to call it a day and resort to custard pie fights in the bar; such was the case with the Annual Squadron Dinner at RAF Wittering, to which myself and fellow Sim' operators had been invited. As for work, I'm still the hapless Simulator instructor on the Harrier - an aircraft I have never flown yet I'm supposed to set emergencies and debrief 'top gun' jet jocks on what they've done wrong. They at least treated me politely, but the annual Christmas lunch was an event that made me realise, I was in a boy's club and for once everyone wanted to be in it.

Halfway through the meal - I'm not sure who started it - but the super soakers appear as if from nowhere and water is rained down upon the four or five Navy seconded pilots from at least five or six of these high pressure devices; retaliation is swift in the form of fairy liquid bottles but then out comes the secret weapon unveiled from below the mahogany table and from the depths of a Naval holdall - they've made a bazooka from an old cardboard tube and are - what are they doing? Lighting the end of it? Suddenly water cascades down from the top table - it's the Station Commander no less, who's supposed to remain impartial; the four gold rings on his mess kit standing out in the fog of battle unleashing the full blast of a hurriedly commandeered super soaker in an attempt to extinguish this infernal Naval device. The heroic duo re-target their devilish contraption right at the Station Commander's table despite the onslaught of cakes, buns and at least ten streams of high pressure liquid bearing down on them from all angles, surely I am witnessing the very stuff of Trafalgar, Taranto and Jutland all at once - there is the sound of discharged explosive, a large cabbage careers through the air impacting the wall behind the Station Commander's head and his large mahogany table is immediately upended by himself and OC Operations, deciding they need solid wood protection from such devices. The Naval duo have been reinforced by a couple of other Naval bazooka makers and have decided to make it a frontal assault on the opposing table - us - and we are only armed with vol au vents and sausage rolls. 'Bang' goes the mixture of fertiliser and bleach (amongst other things) and more cabbage leaves and newspaper rain down on us. My lasting image is the sight of our illustrious Station Commander, A Group Captain, a Harrier pilot of many thousands of hours no doubt, peering over his upended wooden blockade trying to return fire whilst being drenched by a pilot officer standing twenty feet away with a perfectly ranged Super Soaker. Carnage. But it felt like Christmas, and for once the kids were missing out. I thought such things would always be the case.

Needless to say, it is impossible to ever witness any such thing again; the armed forces ability to momentarily break down all authority and laugh at itself is very healthy. You might think it's juvenile, perhaps it is. But twenty four hours a day the RAF follows the rule of status and rank continually whilst knowing full well that it's a game that needs to be played. To switch off and pelt your senior officer with cakes, water and cabbages for half an hour is the greatest aid to leadership we've ever developed.

Chapter 35

Sudden loss

The snoring was loud as I shared an airless, sweaty, hastily constructed room with two other crew members trying to sleep before taking off to Saudi Arabia and the first Gulf War re-supply, once again at daybreak. Where else would you find yourself having to share a room with two older guys, navigating the dark, wet, fly-ridden toilets at midnight having flown an aircraft for ten hours to an airbase in the middle of the med'? But the dusty, fly-ridden billet was a great leveller and I couldn't help but be impressed at the way these veterans just bedded down and accepted this smelly, non-air-conditioned shack as their roof for the night.

We'd taken a few metal chairs out onto the yard outside the billets and had a few beers before turning in. Not me though, as you know by now I didn't really drink. For some reason I had no wish to be sucked into what I saw as an escape from boredom; I also thought I might not be able to stop if I got a taste for it, but it also meant I never really relaxed or appreciated just whom I was with, like the two in the room I was with right now.

The Captain I'd known for several years and we had both, on the odd occasion, waved at his family from two thousand feet as we circled over his farm and horses on the way back from the odd low level flight, I'd also once forgotten to raise the flaps as we departed from a parachute drop zone, resulting in an overstress report that he'd had to make...

'Not one of your better trips Laurie' was all he had to say for the point to have been made stronger than any cursed, stiff rebuke.

You just didn't want to let this fatherly gentleman down. On one trip the crew had sipped Retsina and eaten Cyprian Mezzes in the famous 'Eagles Nest' high on the hill above Limassol where they served 24 course meals, which of course I didn't partake of because I was a pseudo vegetarian and could only eat the Calamari; nevertheless, as he sampled his wine and joked with the gathered crew in the warm December open air, what would have been just another trip to Cyprus he compared to a Martini weekend where we pretended the relentless schedule of 14 hours on, 14 hours off, wasn't so bad; it was instead a weekend away in the Mediterranean and we were living the life. What a great way to look at things.

The Navigator was doing the snoring; he was known for his quiet exactitude with reference to figures and times, which was why he used to work for the 'special' flight; the reasoned manner with which he went about advising the Captain of his next heading, fuel state required, possible diversions and the simple courteous way in which he would treat everyone equally on the flight deck – like a gent in an exclusive men's dining club as he passed on his essential information with an observance of manners that matched his observance of mathematical detail.

It was a pleasure to be flying with these two and I didn't deserve it, but that's the nature of flying a Hercules; you had no idea who you were going to make the next trip with; each time it was a different crew and you might suddenly have to spend a week, even a month with them if you break down somewhere like Diego Garcia in the Indian Ocean (a week of hell). I was comparatively inexperienced but these two allowed me to do my job without a single cynical comment; no judgment on my annoying dietary habits or my obsessive adherence to running every morning, and I appreciated their quiet acceptance of what came their way; it was yet another example to me of how the truly excellent in this world don't wear it on their sleeve, aren't often arrogant and don't need to prove anything – they've already done it.

I didn't realise as I tried to sleep in that hot, airless, Akrotiri rest room amidst those older, experienced guys that this would be the last trip I made with them, the last time I would work with them. Not long after they were both killed in a tragic flying accident whilst on a low level training mission in Scotland. Two of the most accurate aircrew I'd known, If it could happen to them it would have happened to me, and even though the Herc' is a pretty safe aircraft, when one goes in a lot of great people go with it. I just didn't happen to be on that trip. I wish I'd had a drink with them every time it had been offered.

Chapter 36
Pushing the envelope

With the Captain's hand on the throttles we descended towards this pathetically short strip of dirt dug out of the side of a remote mountain in northern Iraq. American Spec' forces were waiting for us as we were one of the first planes to try and land on what appeared to be a dirty footpath – but the graphs in the performance manual said we could do it - just - so we were trusting our lives to several straight lines on graph paper and a list of performance figures to make sure the aircraft could land and take-off from this strip.

The funny thing was, it couldn't.

The strip was too short to legally land and take off – the air was so thin at this height and it wasn't a runway, it was a pile of rubble knocked hastily out the side of a mountain – in which case (and in true forces style) adopt war time procedures and ignore the figures. Call it MOS – Military Operating Standard – which meant 'do it anyway'. Lose an engine with 90 troops on board and you will just have to go ahead and crash. Risky, but the rules change in wartime.

The dirt strip got closer and closer, I began to make out the odd green-clad figure appearing from sandbags, no one was in the open due to the Kurds taking pot-shots. Soon the mountain was above and we were skimming the hilltops:

'Gear down' said the Captain.

I threw the lever and the hydraulics clanked into action. The Herc' must have looked like some approaching vulture that had lost its way as we banked hard amidst this stunningly ruthless landscape of barren hillsides and scattered Kurdish villages. They won't have seen many of these turning up around here.

'Flaps fifty'.

I pulled the flap lever back and the plane ballooned slightly. Captain pulled the throttles back to compensate. A millimetre forward, two millimetres back, the strip stayed constantly in front, getting bigger. If we didn't hit the first few feet right on target we'd overshoot and be a fireball. Size of a football field. Too short, far too short.

'Flaps to full'.

I lowered landing flap that gave us two big barn doors to slow us down to threshold speed.

We hit the dirt - and rocks – at about a hundred and twenty knots – about 130 mph, the Captain slammed the throttles into reverse and we hung on our straps as the engines tried to slow us down with a roar that announced our arrival – dust and dirt was thrown forward and all was suddenly obliterated in a fog of brown.

Men appeared wearing helmets and large goggles, weapons strung round their backs waving batons, they seemed to know what they were doing; the engineer and Nav' were busy sorting out fuel states and our route back; down the back the Loadie was busy chucking on Marines who shuffled up the back ramp with rucksacks bigger than a man and strapped themselves in.

It was that quick, and that desperate, in minutes we were ready to go again.

The men in goggles ran back to their sandbags as I set the throttles and looked at the strip in front that looked no longer than my old school's miniscule football pitch, the one who's centre circle almost touched the penalty area.

'Not much is it?' Said the Engineer.

'Take off power'.

'Set'.

Feet firmly on the brakes, the only thing holding us back from oblivion. Make sure we have all the power the engines have got before we commit. Flight engineer, me and the Captain triple check those lines of engine gauges to see if one, just one, is giving us a clue as to a forthcoming engine failure. This check could save all our lives...

The Allison turbo-props pulled at the brakes as our combined weight pressed down on the pedals. We checked every gauge we could see one last time; it was now or never.

I stepped off the brakes - slowly, painfully slowly she began to roll like an unwieldy mobile house. 'Rolling' I called, wishfully.

Around us sat the beautifully passive Iraqi mountains six thousand feet below the strip, waiting, just waiting to accept us and our oblivion, If we lost an engine on take-off we wouldn't be able to climb, we'd have to crash - our final resting place would be amidst the barren spikes and hills of northern Iraq.

Slowly she began to roll slightly faster – the cliff edge of certain death just sauntering towards us as we put all our faith in the theory of flight. Air needed to pass over our wings at sufficient speed to cause a suction that resulted in flight. This wasn't idle schoolboy interest any more, this was praying to God that all those calculations, graphs, figures and theories actually worked – we were staking our lives on physics – and I wasn't that sharp at it.

80, 85, 90, 95 knots. We needed 120. I could see the end of the strip getting nearer and the lip of oblivion beyond where the hazy Iraqi landscape waited to claim a few more unfortunate bodies.   100 knots, we didn't have sufficient speed. We waited – 105, we were now unable to stop in time. 110. The runway got shorter, and shorter. 115, 117, a hundred feet of rushing rubble was all there was left as we forced with the power of our collective minds those last few knots from the dial in front.

'Rotate' he called.

I pulled back, he kept the throttles at maximum as the props clawed their way off the dirt. But she wasn't lifting. We were too heavy. I kept pulling, he kept the throttles straining at the gauges. The cliff edge went beneath us, somehow we were airborne, hanging, straining, sinking, sinking...no - slowly climbing...? Troops, hot evening air, tons of aluminium and those life-saving Allison turbo-props slowly dragged the complaining overweight, over-fed airframe into the thin air and evening sky. Pot shots, angry Kurds and a front line world left impossibly behind.

It wasn't over. We waited and watched. Engineer's hands microscopically adjusting each power lever whilst monitoring each and every gauge as we watched the air speed reach our safety speed of 162 knots. At that speed we could survive and fly on three engines if necessary – a legal requirement – normally.   There it was – the beautiful figure of 162. Life. We're alive. The evening opened up and we were ready to think of the future once again. We were airborne, the mountains below – to anyone watching it looked like everything was fine, gauges good and everyone doing their job – but at any moment the plane could have lost that engine…

We carried on climbing.   The engines kept roaring.

'Cyprus weather's good' Came the Nav'. 'Estimating Akrotiri at 2230.'

'Beers at 2300' added the Flight Engineer.

'Nice work gang' muttered the Captain over the intercom; it was a quiet but heartfelt mutter. As a team we inwardly nodded and set about breathing again.   Captain later got a Mention in Despatches for this trip.

Loadie's voice comes over the intercom:

'The Marine Officer is complaining that his men haven't got any ear defenders'

Can't get everything right I guess.

Chapter 37

I buy a Capri

Oh I'm so tired of being ripped off when it comes to cars, and there it was just outside the airfield gates - a Ford Capri - gunmetal blue - mag wheels - long bonnet like a Spitfire - the icon of the 70s/80s and just sat there waiting in the front garden as I turned my internally rusted Citroen 2CV6 for home. I kept driving past the beast as I went in each morning, no internal rust on a Ford, good wheels, maybe the engine's good too. 700 quid. Amazingly cheap, and I needed a car.

Of course I was suspicious and knew all the tricks because most of them had already been played on me - the rust on the Citroen, the welding on the VW, the speedo that didn't work on the GTi, the lights that flickered. Nope, not this time. This time I turned up to meet the owner with my checklist.

They seemed a reasonable, middle aged couple that I joked with 'well I know where to find you if it's a pile of rubbish!' We all laughed. I looked underneath, had a torch - oh yes - looking for that welding that needed doing, looking for those holes with flaky brown bits. Nothing. Engine started beautifully, 1600 sounded fine, lights - every one of them worked - check the indicators - all of them - yep.

'Go for a drive?' Sure shrugged the owner, as if it was so perfect there was no need but - hell - if you really want to. He let me drive it - didn't want to accompany me - clearly trusted me. I felt honoured, must be the RAF flying suit, I thought. She drove like a ten year old Capri, pretty darn good as I swerved it around the back lanes and country roads surrounding Lyneham. I went through my list; electrics; check, underside; check, tyres; great, all the dials - work, oil, petrol, battery, fine. Spare tyre and repair kit - all in order.

I pulled up in their garden and stood back and looked her over, checked the tax, MOT, all good. Gunmetal blue Ford Capri, I could see anything wrong. I'll take it. £700, cash. So easy, for once I have a steal. I hop in and race it around to a friend's - jump in! I shout. He bounces down the path and goes to open the door, can't open it. He pulls, still won't open. I push the door, kick the door, play with the handle, try unlocking it, still won't open. 'You just bought a car with the passenger door welded shut'.

Bloody hell readers, the Viz character of Terry Fuckwit springs to mind. Two years of friends having to climb in the passenger window, or sliding across the seat from the driver's side. Couldn't get in contact with the owners.

I make an addition to the checklist.

Chapter 38

Aero-modeller imposter

Returning to the bar at the Akrotiri Officer's Mess in Cyprus wasn't the glamourous thing that it sounds. Most evenings were like a Sunday anywhere else. Usually empty, maybe a few tired looking middle-aged guys perched on bar stools, one playing the one armed bandit in the corner, the chink of snooker going on in the room next door, gin and tonics, pints of cheap beer, faded paint, a pervasive sense of emptiness; suddenly we're all stuck up on cheap high stools listening to war stories; but every now and then, into this staging post would come old acquaintances from my flying training days - and tonight was one of them. It took me back to my days at Linton on Ouse and basic jet training...

It was embarrassing.

There we were standing around in the Officer's Mess bar with our newly acquired uniforms waffling on about how brilliant we were at flying and how this course would just be a breeze and we'd be flying Phantom interceptor jets within a year. But one chap stood awkwardly with his pint and had a head too small for his lanky, uncoordinated body:

'I've been flying a lot in the last year - mostly control line - over a hundred hours at least.'

What? How did he afford that? Here we are just arrived at RAF Linton on Ouse and ready to start two years of intense flying training and this guy looking down on me is claiming, at nineteen years old, that he's well experienced already? One piece of his information didn't fit in:

'What do you mean 'Control Line?'

He scrunched his face into a concentrated ball and without a hint of self-consciousness explained:

'Model aircraft - control line model aircraft.'

I can't believe he said that, I felt like giving him a slap and telling him to grow up. Of course we had all played with model aircraft in our youth - I had myself had been a keen aero modeller of the infamous 1/72nd scale plastic non-flying variety; I had tried flying models but either the wings immediately 'clapped hands' - i.e.: folded up, or else I ran out of glue and never finished them. One remained on top of my wardrobe for about ten years before I covered it in tissue paper and launched it impatiently into the sky - whereupon it described a beautiful arc that started with my hand and ended abruptly nose first, full power into the ground.

'Yes I've entered many aerobatic competitions.' Gushed the nineteen year old with his pint held awkwardly in a hand that looked like it had been better used scribbling essays.

My eyes didn't even flicker, to save embarrassment I merely pretended I was on the same track and deftly switched to talking about the subject he thought we were talking about – model aircraft flying. 'I prefer radio control gliders myself' I was an immediate expert and leant against the bar to humour myself. 'Yes but Control Line flying is so much more exciting'.

In the corner of the Linton on Ouse bar a cheer went up as someone probably downed his pint faster than someone else.

'So how much actual flying have you done – how many hours?'

'Oh hundreds'.

'I mean real flying - as in aircraft that you actually sit in and pilot?

He didn't flinch, just shrugged his shoulders; 'None at all', came the reply from the awkward, fresh-faced nineteen year-old pilot trainee, and he went back to the subject of aerobatics with model aircraft.

Well that's settled then; I realised this gawky kid had somehow mistakenly slipped through the net and that the selectors of pilots had let in a keen aero-modeller hobbyist under the mistaken notion that when he talked about 'going solo' and aerobatic sequences they thought he meant doing it in a real aircraft. How embarrassing, I thought, bought what was probably the second pint of beer he'd ever tasted and made an excuse to be the other side of the bar with the beer contest amidst my usual gathering of world-weary twenty year-old trainee pilots.

It was seven years later, those days of fresh-faced enthusiasm for an undiscovered world of flight had been replaced by eyes of world weary monotony and fear of relentless 'route checks' to unknown countries. I was in the always empty Officer's mess bar in Cyprus; it was long after the Gulf War had ceased to have any newsworthy impact but we were still flying backwards and forwards to keep them stocked up with toilet rolls and land rovers. The bar in Akrotiri was a place resembling a soon-to-bederelict, downtrodden council estate house with faded prints of Lancasters and Sunderland aircraft on the walls, with the Navigator and Captain sat isolated on the high bar-stools discussing riveting subjects such as how much they had drunk in Washington last year, how Gin and Tonic can prevent Malaria, what escapades so and so had got up to *last* time they were here... when in he walks, the aero-modeller; confidently loping into the whitewashed bar with a few of his mates; but far from having the thousand yard stare of the Herc' crew with several thousand hours gazing out at a blue sky, he seemed alive, interested, as if they'd just driven in from Limmassol rather than fly several hours from the UK.

'So how you getting on?' I asked once the handshakes were out of the way.

'Hawks - just landed- one night and we're off again, we're off to check out Limmasol - know any good bars?'

 Hawks? Fast jets? Hurtling around the sky in the same sleek, fun aerobatic masterpiece the red arrows use and he was just as enthusiastic, just as keen about flying as that time in the bar way back in Linton on Ouse in '84. I looked around at my fellow middle aged, bloated crew members in their polo shirts staring around trying to pass the time, pointing fingers and chucking out cod philosophy, I scanned the faded pictures, noted the flower outside the window was bright pink as nature reminded me of a thing or two, the one armed bandit flickering and flashing in the corner and I knew this bar would probably be the same in ten years' time, and I might still be here, hearing the same stories on this eternal Sunday evening.

Yeah, I know a few' I replied.

He looked at the fellow disinterested crew-members ensconced around the bar, quickly realising that I was one of them.

'Still flying the model aircraft?   I asked with a half-smile, by way of distraction.

'Of course' came the assertive, confident reply.

He half-glanced my company, noted the surroundings and had the decency not to ask me.

Chapter 39

The end of the eighties – and a medal

Back at Lyneham I was called into the Wingco's office. It was 1990, and my dreams at the start of the eighties were very different from those at the end as I knocked on the cheap wooden door.

I put my head round the corner, he didn't look up; buried in some admin' niff-naff surrounded by magi-boards of hastily written felt tip and a framed photo of a Victor tanker. Your worth as a pilot was often measured as to how sharp and pointed was the aircraft you used to fly before you ended up here. The office had a musty atmosphere that probably hadn't changed in forty years of fidgety Wing Commanders pushing paper about who'd rather be out there flying. What they didn't need were annoying twats like me who didn't quite fit in and couldn't be pigeonholed - like they had been.

'You wanted to see me - sir?'

'Catch' he mumbled distractedly, and threw the small box at me; he was back at his form filling in before it had even landed in my hands.

Later on I opened the blue cardboard container; inside were yellow and blue ribbons, some design of a gun, an anchor and eagle. It had substance, heavy, clearly well made. All I could think was that I hadn't earned it. I thought of the soldiers and tank crews who'd sustained the blood, sweat and tears whilst here I was back in sunny Wiltshire - some of them were still out there - for ever - certainly lots of conscripted Iraqis. But then I thought about the trips I'd made from front-line Saudi airfields suffering the Scud attacks we thought might annihilate us with lethal blood agent, and then found myself landing back in UK and shopping in the local village Gateway supermarket in the evening, the risky take-off in Sirsenk, the 2am re-supply take-offs to Akrotiri, the ten hour long hauls and the 75 trips to Cyprus back to back...

You've all got short memories. So easy to laugh and think 'you mug' and say 'what air force?' when I mention Iraq; but if you could see the wider public when this war broke out, when Saddam invaded Kuwait, when the oilfields were threatened in Saudi; there was a real fear of what he would do to captured aircrews, what the unknown Imperial Guard were going to be like against our own troops. Yes, now you laugh and say what did you have to worry about? There was no blood agent. no nuclear arsenal, no WMD... but when we were going out there we all had no idea, we thought we might get shot down, nuked, biological warfare was a genuine threat, Saddam might win, airfields might be overrun whilst we were refuelling. Until we started watching the cruise missiles on TV blowing up the hangars we had no idea. Yeah, well that is when I was making all those trips, with crews chain smoking and drinking, marriages breaking up because of the nerves; hindsight allows us to see the irony, the imbalance between the two sides; but at the time the country wanted people to head out there quickly and sort it out - and I had volunteered and been paid a fat wage for many years just so you could rely on me to stand up and be counted out there. I say this because the level of cynicism that I come across these days is annoying; when Saddam started rattling his sabre everyone appeared scared as to what might happen; we waited, watched the forces do their aggressive, rather distastefully violent sort of thing, win (luckily). Then everyone started complaining about it being too easy, an unequal battle, look what we did to those trucks as they retreated back to Baghdad. But at the time, we were all scared. Scared of what he could do and what he might do later. We forget very quickly.

I thought of the tedium, the lost relationship. Yeah, I'd earned this medal. But never in the way you would have expected. Most people will mock it if they have little intelligence or thought, I will of course mock it because it would look silly to wear my one medal, or to celebrate so many deaths; but it is a symbol of my efforts.

The eighties, that had started in a Portsmouth disco with my mate telling me through the booming bass that it was a new decade, that it was 1980 - something we weren't used to - had now come to an end - and I was ten years older. But my days in the RAF were easier to quantify - they had begun with me in a grey belted boiler suit, marching up and down in those hangars - yeah I'd come a long way.

I was secretly proud, whatever others may think; you've read some of what I've been through and may dismiss it as trivial and pointless. Many do, it's fashionable. I only wore the medal once to an Air Cadet parade, and it looked ridiculous. The fifteen year old Corporal couldn't help smirking - because he was fifteen - he knew no better. One medal... my Granddad had several more from the Somme and Loos, but he never talked about it.

I'd come out at the end of the eighties scarred; the balloon jump, the wings, the Hercules thing hadn't worked out in my opinion because I wasn't a Captain - whether I wanted to be one or not wasn't the question - but some truly enjoyable moments had occurred and yet faced with the end of my tour as a co-pilot I was beginning to think that perhaps there were new challenges out there.

Chapter 40

Surrounded in Sarajevo

'Ah, Monsieur Le Tallack' called my Swiss downstairs neighbour (in her nineties) as I passed her on the stairs in my flying suit and flight case (my initials are L. E. Tallack - she thought I was of French extraction - which I quite liked) 'do you know the gas man is calling on Monday - are you going to be in?' I shook my head and suppressed a snigger - 'I'm - not sure ' I muttered as I hopped in my battered Citroen 2CV6 (another one, don't ask) and made off from Bath for the regular weekend trip via Lyneham to the Bosnian conflict of the mid-1990s.

I pull into a garage to fill up with petrol, as I get out the car a woman calls across to me 'fill 'er up with four star please' she thinks I'm a petrol pump attendant dressed, clearly not like a US Navy Pilot in Top Gun, but as a ragged RAF pilot in a bunch of overalls. It was an understandable mistake.

But in the midst of these reminders to a regular life, our trip on this Saturday morning was to fly in to war torn Sarajevo, deliver whatever we had to deliver and get out again as soon as possible. The City was still under siege from sniper fire and the buildings were suffering the results of artillery fire. We had armoured seats, armoured head rests that curved round our heads, armoured seat pans; and we were carrying reporters and cameramen with us, who all got a bit worried when they suddenly saw us twenty miles out from Bosnia, put down our chicken curry, stow our cups of tea and start to put on Kevlar bullet proof vests and helmets.

As we came into view of Sarajevo airport what I thought was cloud I realised was in fact smoke - drifting out of the tops of the ruins of one time recent flats, houses, hotels; not a single building was intact but instead smoke rising from recent direct hits drifted across the runway and reminded that this was very much still an active warzone and we were a great hulking target slamming down in the middle of it with low visibility markings; perhaps we were fair game too?

There was rumour of sniper activity hence the armour protection, and as we taxied in and stopped on the wide open concrete pan I was faced with a panoramic view of what a city looks like when its suffered constant mortar attack, artillery shells and civilians have been picked off by snipers; it doesn't look natural, it looks like some giant has taken a bite out of it and no one's at home other than the sort of people you'd really rather avoid.

'Keep her on the brakes Co' says the departing Captain, and with the rest of the crew he quickly scarpers from the flight deck, leaving me alone, a sitting duck for any sniper, stamping on the brakes and holding an entire four engined aircraft stationary whilst the props spun and the Allisons whined. It takes quite a bit of effort, but at the same time I kept ducking my head and bobbling about like a hyper-active glove puppet in case a well-aimed bullet suddenly whistled through the non-bulletproof windshield. Or perhaps he'd go for a centre of mass shot - stomach shot - I quickly wriggled in my seat, leant back, leant forward - perhaps he was getting tired trying to track me with his cross hairs and decided to try other, easier prey.

Perhaps I was drawing attention to myself by moving about so much. Stop moving, quick - move erratically. To any bystander I must have looked like I had St Vitus dance. I had so much kit in my pockets which might deflect the bullet - my life-saving passport (doubtful), life-saving car keys, life-saving trusty wallet; the flimsy Kevlar vest didn't exactly fill me with confidence. But let's face it, coming under sniper fire is not something many people live to talk about; either they're lining up the shot on you, and miss, which means you probably never even know he took a shot - or you definitely know about it for about a millisecond before you die. So who knows how dangerous it was.

Needless to say, I survived the non-existent sniper (or perhaps he was just a really bad shot), so we unloaded, taxied quickly to the runway intersection to save time and stuck all four engines on full power as we rounded the corner onto the main strip, straightened out with the engines kicking out all they had and dragging us into the air and out of that smoking ruin before we became too obvious.

We were in and out of there in about ten minutes, leaving the burning buildings way behind and below us before a two hour flight back via Italy and France to the ever-peaceful Lyneham, a drive through the Wiltshire countryside and down into the Palladian architecture of Bath and the Jane Austen surroundings of Camden Crescent - my flat looked down on the rooftops and the church spires and I could wander down to the corner shop where handmade cakes and fine wine were sold opposite the pub that had live jazz every night. Had I really been wearing a bullet proof vest and dodging (potential) sniper fire three hours ago? All the roofs intact, the Swiss lady downstairs, late afternoon Saturday shoppers make their way up the Lansdowne road as always and no one would even think there's a war on just a couple of hours away.

Looks like I'll be in time for the gas man after all...

Chapter 41

Who do you know?

Not all the Bosnia trips were scheduled.   Ten months before I had booked a weekend off - and I might indeed have the weekend off anyway - but I wanted to guarantee it because two of my rare civilian friends were getting married; both of them had stayed friends with myself and Pip despite our gallivanting individually around the world on a regular basis for weeks on end, which was impressive, so I thought I should at least make the effort for this.

Phone rings - Friday evening before the wedding - 'Squadron Leader XXX here - the Co-pilot's gone ill and you're the duty replacement - report for Bosnia trip tomorrow morning.'

I phone back...

'Sir, I understand the order and all - but I did book leave ten months ago so I shouldn't be on standby crew'.

'Well you're down as duty replacement crew...'

'That is surprising - and it's a friend's wedding that I booked last year...'

'Well in that case they'll understand - and if they don't they can't be much of a friend... now stop arguing and do as you're told. '

That's the sort of shit you get handed by a squadron leader - not only a callously stupid remark about your private relationships, but a clear mistake in the planning roster - there's no doubt that I'll do what I'm told, I just wanted to point out that it's a mistake.

The phone goes down, I've made my point, I pack my bags and cancel my plans for tonight's stag do. I'll also await the one-way interview on Monday morning.

An hour later the phone rings again.

'Tallack - who do you know?'

It's the Squadron Leader again, genuinely quizzical and dumbfounded.

'Sorry sir?

'Who do you know to pull these strings?'

'I'm sorry I don't understand sir'

'Flight Lieutenant XXX has just volunteered to take the Co-pilot's seat out of nowhere - he's a Captain - does he owe you a favour?'

Needless to say, post wedding and Monday morning, I'm called into the Squadron Leader's office;

'What the hell do you think you're doing arguing with me?'

'I just thought it unreasonable that I book one day off in all the years I've been in the RAF and it gets cancelled at the last minute - it's not as if there's a war on.

Bad move, I fell into his trap.

'This *is* a bloody war!'

Yep - he's right - Bosnia is an actual war. I was - almost - dodging sniper fire just the other day.

I meant to clarify that our country wasn't under threat, but thought his face was red enough and he had a point. And that's the forces for you; anything you hold sacred like a mate's wedding - your own wedding - isn't guaranteed. You might be called away for anything - which sounds romantic and exciting from my position now; but in reality, when it's regularity you crave- a night school class - a date at a critical time, a phone call you need to make - all these things take a back seat. For crew members with families the Herc' provided a welcome escape and release before a heroic return and renewed energy with the family. But I was beginning to think that this very lifestyle was stopping me from actually achieving that very family - or regular friends, girlfriends (hardly any), family, Christmas, New Year, the seasons. It got in the way of everything every year.

The reason the Captain took my place?

Unknown to the Squadron Leader, the Captain who volunteered was having a thing with the female navigator. I just wish he'd been ten minutes faster. Hooray for mixed gender flight decks.

Chapter 42

Cup of tea, then out the door and into battle

Four hours we'd been up, at night, circling five miles high over the Isle of Man in total darkness on a hot summer Saturday night army exercise. It was 1am and almost time to do our bit.

A couple of Parachute regiment officers (yes, one's a Major, but I seemed to get on with this one), roughly dressed in para smocks, were quietly chatting with us in the red, soporific glow of the flight deck, sipping soup and eating pies heated up for them by the Loadie as we sat seemingly stationary, high above a blackened world outside in the confined space of droning engines and small adjustments being made here and there by the flight engineer whilst he ate a pasty and we all quietly went on with our separate businesses. They were clearly struck by the droning silence. We nodded, pointed to the odd gauge, let them know the temperature down there, the forecast, wind speed. It was the peaceful hum of quiet expectancy you might experience in a taxi rank office or the staff room of a coach depot, everyone knew their jobs and monitored the radar screen (Nav), the fuel gauges (Eng), the radio (Co), the cargo hold and food (Loadie) The Para' officers - Colonels, Majors, their radio operator, acted as our poetic observers as this seemingly domestic arrangement of five men in clean overalls eating, drinking and supposedly flying, oblivious to the deafening noise from the engines, navigated this darkened room to where they needed to go. .Now and then the Colonel would confer with his radio operator down in the cargo bay as the rest of his parachute assault went in ahead of them a few hundred miles away in the Outer Hebrides.

'Well, guess it's time we were off, thanks for everything.'

It's not often your Saturday night visitors decide to go home by way of parachute, but it was the Colonel's time to join the war; these seemingly passive, well-mannered chaps sipped the remains of their soup, finished their pies, thanked us for the stay on the flight deck and the lift up to some barren island in the Outer Hebrides as they donned helmets and clambered down the back into the cargo hold.

The glowing red, Aladdin's Cave of a cockpit might have been stationary for all you could see, but we'd gradually brought her down to over a Scottish island at 800 feet and 120 knots - we were on the drop zone. We relayed a message to the Colonel, his fellow officer and his radio operator - five minutes. I say 'apparently' because he had no way of knowing, he just took our word for it; there was the flickering light of the DZ, we got a call, the Nav confirmed we were in the right place, checked the wind, outside was blackness, just a radar altimeter telling us 800 feet and a tiny light winking at us on the ground.

'Red on' called the Nav.

I pushed the light switch to red.

We could feel the rush of air as the Loadie opened the cargo door.

A pause in the darkness, we'd just spent Saturday night with these people.

'Green on' called the Nav.

I pushed the light switch to green.

They were gone. On our word all three had just jumped into pitch blackness, completely trusting this team of five people they'd never met before. It seemed unreal that they weren't here.

The cargo bay was empty, the Loadie closed up.

'Three canopies', confirmed the Loadie.

And they were far away below us, clumping down into who knows what.

That impressed me.

Chapter 43

Captaincy?

It's approaching the end of my two year tour of duty on 70 Squadron; I'd worked hard during the Gulf war, passed the relentless six monthly and six weekly tests, successfully completed the low level course and even got a medal. I'd done nothing wrong apart from not drink, be a pain in the neck fussy eater and messed up that one trip to Exeter after two solid weeks of flying to the Gulf and back. Others had smashed up motorbikes, crashed their cars in the mess car park, insulted Akrotiri Operations Commanders, been found in a ditch outside Limmasol and flown between two hotels on Mombasa beach and terrified the President. I thought I'd been pretty well behaved, comparatively speaking.

So it was a little bit of a surprise to be told by my boss that it wasn't going to happen. I asked why - was it just that one moment on Exeter approach two years ago? No. My past? The bulimia? I got a subtle nod. But I'm A1 G1 Z1 now, I'd been assured that was now behind me and I had a clean slate when I arrived on the Squadron. The flight commander shook his head behind the moustache; 'Sorry'.

Sod. I felt like an eating disorder had come back to haunt me.

Yeah maybe, maybe I hadn't been that popular, maybe I'd made some bad decisions, hadn't exuded Captaincy material. Let's face it, I'm not trying to blame this on any one thing. No excuses and no 'if only' - they'd decided. In which case all I could do was learn from it, I was going to have to face another tour on another squadron as a co-pilot. So be it. Serves me right. But who'd have thought that the very thing I'd been doing to maintain my health; running and eating carefully, had perhaps resulted in my practically losing a career.

Chapter 44

Low Level Luck

I've got two Hercs behind me and we're hurtling along at low level approaching a turning point and I've got no idea if we're gonna see it, if I miss it we're lost and her majesty's formation of three troop carrying aircraft fully laden with a total of 270 paratroopers are going to be swanning about, low level above the Cotswolds disturbing farmers and village cricket matches having got lost in the first ten minutes. Would I see the turning point? Why had I chosen a cross roads that I couldn't see unless I was actually over it?

As you already know by now, I wasn't particularly popular as a Co-pilot; I didn't drink and spent the rest of my time long distance running due to an obsession with weight brought about by watching everyone else eat four meals a day whilst immovably lodged in the Hercules cockpit. I'm not saying that was the only reason, but after being given the green light after my eating disorder I spent a year and a half slogging away quite successfully as a Co-pilot before being told I wasn't going to be put forward for Captaincy. It was annoying. I felt duped. I also had a check ride leading a three- ship formation of Hercules at low level with a couple of hundred paratroopers to drop.

Suddenly it all seemed pointless, as acting Copilot on this trip I had more to do than the Captain – I needed to plot the route, prepare the maps and brief the crews – but I already roughly knew the route we'd take and anyway, I'd just been told all my hard work over the last eighteen months had been for nothing. My Captain – the Wingco – didn't appreciate my breezing in to flight planning whilst the others had been planning for an hour or so before me and quickly drawing a line on a map, jotting down a few numbers and then standing up to give a briefing to the assembled crews of the route. Oh, and by the way, it was my annual check ride so there was another Captain watching over me; the Wingco was watching, hoping the checker would spot my slackness of attitude, but I was carefully letting it be seen only by the old enemy – plus, what the old buzzard didn't know, the checker had flown with me for two weeks solid during the Gulf war, but I didn't want to look an idiot in front of him.

We'd taken off as a three ship, checked in, turned onto the first heading and settled down to droning across the north Wiltshire countryside at 250 feet; I gripped the multi coloured map loosely in my left hand whilst changing frequencies with the other.

'See that pylon on the horizon?'

'Er – yep' Came the reply.

'Head for that'.

It was a grey, low cloud, late afternoon and the visibility up ahead was getting misty, hazy, rain spattered the windscreen as we drifted past cross roads and Bath stone pubs I wished I knew the name of, because we'd been following the right heading, offset for wind, stopwatch running, but right now I had no idea whether the cross roads – our critical first turning point – was up ahead or not. I couldn't see it, visibility was poor and I'd bloody well gone and chosen a cross roads on a hill top–

something you couldn't see unless you were right over it. Twat. The two Hercs behind were manned by highly competent co- pilots who answered my calls efficiently and immediately – they trusted me:

'One minute to turn'

But I had no idea where we were, to the onlooker on the ground we must have looked like three beautiful, majestic grey birds that heaved and swayed their bulk to the sound of roaring turboprops as they went about their daring mission to who knows where – when in fact we were three giant, blind behemoths blundering along into the cloud of doom led by a bloody idiot.

I thought about the mass of hardware hurtling across the English countryside, three giant cargo planes had somehow become reliant on my leadership as I sat sweating and thinking – how long before I start going 'er...just circle round a bit could you?'

The Wingco sat next to me fully anticipating and no doubt relishing a fuck up – he just steered the Herc on the heading I gave him and kept her at 250 feet on the radar altimeter, old checker friend leant between us. I didn't move, adopted casual seated position of map in one hand, radio in other, casually looking across the increasingly darkening fields whilst my eyes searched desperately for a bloody crossroads somewhere out there amongst the moonscape of Bath stone villages and anonymous fenced off fields of carefree cattle. I almost sensed the Wingco licking his lips in anticipation; 'here we go – the bastard – that'll teach him to turn up to flight planning with just an hour to go, the checker will throw the book at him. I knew it, no wonder he didn't get Captaincy...'

'Ten seconds to the turn' I call.

'I can't see it' he snaps back.

'Just stay on heading – it'll be a left turn onto 280 degrees in five, four, three (oh hell)

From out the mist emerged miraculously, on the nose, a beautiful summit, completely invisible until actually on top of it, terrible choice of a turning point, with a big, fat, stunningly exposed crossroads that was about to sail beneath us.

'Dead ahead'

Two

One

Turn now...

'Formation turning – turning - now'.

The two Hercs behind acknowledged and turned at thirty second intervals keeping me in sight and relying on me for their navigation. I think only the Wingco was more surprised than me, I seem to remember something approaching the famed 'double take' like they do in cartoons, but I acted as if that had been the plan all along. We rolled on heading on the way to the mountains of Wales and settled in to our sortie. It wasn't long before the cloud hit the deck and we had to pull out of low level and pretty soon cancel the trip and head back to base due to poor weather, but the check ride was still a check ride, and the

Wingco said nothing as we landed, shut the plane down and wandered over to the bar for a late evening debrief.

In front of the non-plussed Wingco the other two Cos came up to me to congratulate me on the navigation:

'Nice one, how the hell did you hit that crossroads on a hilltop!'

'Yeah we were lost as hell and were thinking – hope he knows the way'.

His silence spoke volumes as we sat down in front of the checker with pints of Lager:

'Yeah nice one', the checker murmured between sips, 'you stayed on heading in poor vis' and hit the turning point on time – Obvious you planned this really well - you must have read the visual cues leading up to the turn – in that mist I couldn't make out where we were going. Then the low level pull out – worked as per brief – I don't need to see anymore. You're cleared low level for another year.'

I nodded as if to say, 'of course'.

The Wingco was speechless, pissed off. It didn't fit with his picture of struggling Co-pilots sweating over infinite route details for trips that got cancelled twenty minutes in.

I never let on, just lived on the myth of that seemingly effortless wander in to flight planning, jump in the Herc' and hit a turning point dead on in a zero vis' day and gain a low level qualification in twenty minutes. The Wingco just sat, flew and watched. Might even have wondered about my Captaincy. I had nothing to lose, and it's amazing what can happen when you don't care.

Chapter 45

Don't ask - just carry it

Some strange initials appear on the operations board in capitals – my name is marked in next to them. 'What's that mean?' I ask. Corporal on duty looks from out the corner of her eye, tells me there's a briefing in a few minutes that will explain everything. I wander in to one of our squadron briefing rooms and see the five man crew and a portly Engineering officer with big glasses standing at the front; someone shuts the door. He proceeds to tell us about our trip and what we'll be carrying, how he'll be armed, how it's rather sensitive, how we'll need to leave the aircraft wearing civilian clothing and take a taxi downtown and not talk about it.

I put up my hand.

'What the hell are we carrying?'

He tells me in a vague mutter - as if I don't really need to know, well I'm just the Co-pilot. He quickly changes the subject and then proceeds to tell us how we can all buy duty free and get to the hotel as soon as possible so we don't need to worry about anything.

'Why are we carrying this – and why all the secrecy?'

I feel like I've just farted loudly in front of the Station Commander such is the reaction; I'm not a good reader of Squadron operations briefs but I think I'd have heard about this one. I can't believe he thinks we're a bunch of beer swilling twats who'd carry anything without question 'On Her Majesty's Service' and all that, as if we'll carry arms to the Congo if necessary, just keep us in beer. And anyway, I don't think she knew. I hated this idiot.

The morning came, Police cars swept round the camp roundabout and past the gate guardian of the De Havilland Comet before depositing themselves around the Herc 'on the dispersal; Armed guards were stationed everywhere, we couldn't approach unless in twos, the Engineering officer was there, armed with a Browning 9mm in a shoulder holster, apparently in case one of us went mad and decided to hijack the aircraft – but what would he do? Shoot one of us and fly it himself? I'd like to see him try, but then I found myself asking questions; for instance, as we were deemed trustworthy enough as RAF pilots to fly this mission, why the need for the pistol? It was a strange mixture of sudden trust and sudden readiness to be shot at by my own side, and there he was on the flight-deck, right between us, a keen amateur with the power to terminate. I could have that bloody weapon stripped and in several pieces before he'd worked out how to take the safety catch off.

During the flight he would often lean between us, pretending he was in charge and making pseudo commands and anxious comments if I didn't start level off within two hundred feet of the exact height we were cleared to by Air traffic, or didn't call them at the moment he expected me to, even though I might be checking clearances to enter other airspace or checking the weather at destination, he was nervous and ultimately a liability - dangerous; possessing a little knowledge of flying – which is worse than having no knowledge at all. Worse still he was armed and had probably fired it once in his life during basic training. I wanted to grab the thing out of his silly holster and club him round the head with it, as my potential killer sat between myself and the Captain, like a little child with his toy.

On a later trip – with similar cargo - he made a quip about tree-huggers and 'Save the Whale' types, I told him I thought they had a point, that global warming was a fact, that those types that cared for the environment had my vote.

Over the hotel breakfast next day, perhaps it was because he had been ready to shoot me throughout the flight, or perhaps it was just his educated but morally vacant and abhorrent attitude I'd caught; but I quickly spoke out when he made some predictable quip about Greenpeace and made it very clear that I didn't really care that he was a Squadron leader, I didn't agree with his views on ecology, I dismissed them as typically right-wing, naïve and short sighted. He went silent. Unfortunately I was also sat with the acting Squadron boss at the time; so much for RAF familiarity and lack of rank structure – 'let's all have breakfast together!' So casual... yeah well see what you get, me in your face. The two of them finished their bacon and eggs in thought, yeah go on then, try bloody shooting me.

A day later I was called into the Commanding Officer's office. This guy had a red face with a black crew cut, mid-forties, built like a Rugby prop-forward, he leant over the desk at me and snarled his words:

'Let me tell you I was on 24 hour standby all through the seventies – Vulcans – ready to drop the bomb – and I've got two kids at home'.

Interesting logic but I failed to see his point. I said as much and thought to myself 'who gives a shit?' I had no career and he had me marked me out as a 'leftie', a green-peace activist who didn't believe in war and probably read the Guardian. This was clearly a bollocking. Clearly he assumed I was against war and took drugs and hung with hippies; He was even more red-faced than usual, and he was mistaken; I had no such passivity, I joined fully aware of our potential to destroy large cities; what I objected to was being treated like a Nazi rule follower who'll carry any cargo no questions asked, who'll think all protestors suspect and in the employ of the commies, who'd carry arms to Guatemala if it meant a cheap run to the duty free and heavy drinking by the evening. What an arse.

Air traffic kept us away from all major cities, and after all that to do with guns and Police, they went and scheduled us right over Bath on the way in; there we were, just a few thousand feet from all that Georgian splendour and history, a flying liability.

Chapter 46

The Annual Race

'So you've never won a race?'

He called over as we stood on the line, waiting for the gun.

Okay, so now time to tell you of the sub-plot to my days at Lyneham; when up in the air I might be battling with the egos, binge eating and minimum descent heights, on the ground I'd met a like-minded world of dedicated athletes running the station cross country team - here's one story that summed up the attitude amongst them.

We're all lined up on the starting line, everyone on the station that wants to join the race or can't find an excuse to get out of it, which means there's about two hundred people massing in a mixture of baggy T shirts, RAF regulation shorts and dodgy plimsoles they haven't worn since basic training. But there's also a good smattering of keen runners and racers. I glance along the line and look for the flash running kit – there he bloody is – my arch nemesis and let's face it, faster runner – Stu - grinning away at me, the Army physical training instructor who always bloody beats me. This was one race I'd like to win – in front of a home crowd, my squadron, the base personnel. But it wasn't to be, would it ever be?

I remember telling the Army Sergeant that I'd never actually won a race over a drink once, and he was incredulous, yet here I was supposedly the OIC - Officer in command - Cross Country –

organising races and booking the minibus when I wasn't out of the country flying; we'd all meet once a week to race against the other bases in the local area and I loved it, the wet, windy grass and the sweaty tramping up muddy Wilshire slopes, the hot soup, the escape for an afternoon from the forces; rank meant nothing, we knew each other as Stu, Phil, Andy; I genuinely had no idea as to ranks and for that afternoon, no one cared, you were judged by your speed round the six mile quagmire, a mass of flicking mud-caked legs all trying to keep going and get the highest number of guys through the finish line first.

'Really never won?' He laughed. I knew the ruthless humour of the forces. Put simply, you bonded by taking the piss, which made for some awkward moments when leaving the forces and trying to make friends outside. But if Steve Cramm was on the sidelines commentating he'd be shaking his head and quoting the stats…

'Nope I haven't'.

The starter gun popped like some cap gun in the wind, and we were off. Hundreds of legs all hell for leather, the important thing was not to run with them – they're all excited and will do the first 800 metres in two minutes, then die one by one, and so will I if I get carried away in the moment and go with them. They disappear, bodies much faster than me, myself and Stu and a few others hanging back, ignoring the rush, letting them head off. We head through the uneven airfield grass, trying not to stumble, the tape marked out with spikes marking the route as we're left behind by either super-fit athletes or badly prepared fun runners.

About 800 metres later we drift past the first, then several more, then many more, dead on their feet, their ill-fitting tracksuits giving away their lack of training as we begin to put the pace on, I watch Stu's feet and not long there's about ten of us at the front running around the long grassed airfield perimeter of RAF Lyneham; my squadron boss shouts at me – makes a change – I'm used to him shouting at me but not encouragingly, but there is Stu thirty yards ahead, running in his usual easy style, short steps, legs moving quickly, gaze fixed ten yards ahead. He's pulling slowly away...

One mile to go, I can see the yellow T shorts of my squadron – aircrew aren't exactly known for their fitness but I guess I'm not exactly normal in this place and they're shouting but it's dying down, they've seen the Sergeant ahead of me and the two or three others behind, I should make it in second if I can hang on, just down this tunnel of tape and spikes, so much tape, which way is it? Someone shouts.

We've gone the wrong way.

Stu is fifty yards ahead and turns round.

I've also got the message. Turn round – got thirty yards to backtrack and there're the two others who've also got the message but I might still be able to get in front of them.

Stu is steaming up behind me as I get to the turn and double back to the real finish.

There it is, 300 metres away. Glory.

Stu has caught up at least twenty metres and is now within striking distance as I head for the line, there's a crowd cheering, station commanders, flight line mechanics, Stu is pounding down, I throw my head round – he's fifteen yards behind, I have one hundred metres to go. He's got me. He's caught up too quick. I decide to go anyway. I await his steaming past me. This world is cruel.

He doesn't appear.

I glance around.

He's still fifteen yards behind.

He must be holding it back.

I cross the line to cheers and my own personal triumph. I take the handshakes and collect the medal and plaque. He disappears amidst the crowd. But I seek him out. He's grinning away.

'You bastard – you let me win'.

'No way mate – I was out of it - you won your first race after all', he mutters with a handshake.

To this day I'd like to think I clinched it in that last hundred metres, but I knew his stamina better than I knew him as a person and it was a noble gesture, given that we both went the wrong way; but at the end, as he could see my forlorn attempt at victory about to be thwarted once again, he decided to let it go. My coming exit from RAF had seen at least one major victory.

It'd be twenty years before I'd win another. Thanks Stu.

Chapter 47

Changing Identity

'You're very brave', said my Commanding Officer. He made a phone call. This was to be 'it', and already my superiors were impressed, no more thinking about my failed balloon jump, no more a sense of failure that I'd wound up a Hercules Co-pilot, I was volunteering for Special Work and I was suddenly considered brave, heroic, purposeful and a part of the secretive world we all wanted to be in. What other job lets you watch a few films then gives you the opportunity to live out these fantasies? I say this to let you know how much I wanted to do this, how much every muscle of my body felt it had finally found its purpose...

Pretty soon I was placed in front of a disturbingly attractive WRAF officer (the reward?) who, I'm guessing, was supposed to be asking me questions, but quickly let a few things slip:

'Most seem to have failed at everything else – this is their one big chance to prove themselves. I nodded enthusiastically - even though I didn't really think I'd failed at anything (alright, alright, the balloon jump).

All in the name of proving myself...

'Can I ask how exactly how this would be helping stop the conflict?' She paused, taking me in. 'It's just I wanted to be sure – what exactly I'd be doing.'

From her answer it was obvious that this is what I *should* be doing; as if my whole life had been leading up to it. All that running would have reason once again, my obsessive training would explode with a new sense of purpose; my ability to strip weapons in darkness, cover long distances and all that stuff with maps and mountains would see me suitably messed up in middle age with plenty of war stories. All that climbing, flying, trying to do anything scary; all good harmless fun, unless we get fucked up and start applying to be on units like this and suddenly - it isn't harmless at all - in fact people get downright shot and killed due to nothing more than our urge to prove something. But hey... just my sneaking doubts talking. I bathed in my sudden sense of renewed kudos, Special Ops. That's me. Oh yes, don't like to talk about it you know, followed by a lengthy monologue detailing all the things you can't talk about.

Okay – all good so far – like a splendid meal placed in front of you I surveyed what it consisted of and couldn't believe it's perfection - and when life seems to have given you such perfect opportunity you can't believe it's true, so you want to square it ethically and morally – not always possible in the military but you've signed and sworn an oath so you're in so far; but if I was going to be actually seeking out mayhem, causing potential death and destruction then best I hear the rational answers to what I'm supposed to be fighting for. That was why I asked the question.

Now right here I want you to grant me a massive request; to imagine that I am not what you think I am today – that is, if you know me you'll understand that I'm a grumpy, cynical middle-aged teacher who is nothing more than a better than average runner with a yearning to do something physical once in a while. Instead imagine me a pretty good shot, conversant with most weapons in the UK forces and able to strip an SLR and 9mm Browning in seconds with my eyes shut; yeah I know, boy's own stuff and he's probably just showing off, but hopefully by now you'll have got the message that's the last thing I'm trying to do. I also spent my holidays tramping over Mexico, running up the Brecons and cycling over the Alps in winter. I felt cut out for this.

So imagine for a moment I took this job; in fact anyone writing the story of my life so far - given the information above - would most certainly have had my character jump at this chance – it made complete sense, it wouldn't make sense if I didn't; cue happy ending complete with retirement at 55, house in the country, a cat and a tempestuous blonde wife with adorable offspring, probably working for a well-paid security firm he wandered into through the old boy network, helps out at the local Air Cadets and twice a year heads down to the RAF club to sink a few with his old squadron pals.

So why the hell did I find myself thinking of Bono and Sinead O' Connor? Peaceniks; the complete opposite, but I knew why. Perhaps it was too much watching of 'The Tube', perhaps the 80s musical generation had finally got to me; truth is I don't know, but there was an attitude there, I didn't even know his lyrics, but started listening. There was that far distant stare with the grey album cover with the kid's face somehow stating something stupid about 'peace' – that ridiculous concept - and I'd ignored these voices before; so why now? It's what you're cut out for, you're a soldier and it's what you do.

But then again…

...wouldn't it be something if someone like me started changing? Someone as brainwashed and blindly patriotic as myself, started, just for a moment, thinking about - helping? I hated his vocals, always yelping, Sinead? Well, I admired her ballsy nature, but I always felt they wouldn't like me very much. Anyway, helping? I wouldn't know where to start.

The WRAF officer quietly murmured her response...

'And by your questions I'm not sure you're the sort of person they're looking for.'

Cyprus – callout to the gulf - few days later – I'm on an early run just as the sun was rising and the air is cooler and I'm flitting over the dry earth; suddenly I stop, mid run, and pick up this beautifully simple, yellow flower; I have no idea what it is because I have no time for such things – they don't interest me. Then I think maybe I should start finding out what it is. That evening I fly home.

The boss wandered into the Officer's Mess toilet whilst I was having a pee; awkward moment. I decided to address the point, 'it really wasn't quite what I was looking for.'

He didn't say a word, just finished and went.

I have no idea if people think I got cold feet, it doesn't really matter, but after that I started looking at what we as a country were doing around the world, realised we were still doing it, that I was a part of it so I'd better agree with it, or get out. How could I be doing a job that involved killing people if I wasn't sure we were on the right side? I read somewhere that it was one thing to make a moral mistake, but to keep doing it stops it being a mistake, you become guilty. There was voluntary redundancy being offered.

I'm a great believer in the myth of the person who says 'well it was either me or them' - no it wasn't, because I was actively trying to put myself there in the first place where I'd potentially be faced with just that situation. And why? Because of a need to prove myself, nicely camouflaged under the flag of the forces? So that I can turn to you now in some bar and say I have real status rather than the rather lack-lustre status I actually have, where alpha males talk about hush hush missions - so that I can feel one with them? So as a result people have to die - for my ego. Woh. Wait a minute. Believe me, I have suffered the comments of people who've never been near the forces, who say - 'Oh I get it you just got out because you weren't a Captain then', have taken the back seat in conversations about military prowess when, perhaps, if I made use of my fitness, my regiment background, my comprehensive knowledge of weapons, perhaps that all might have changed.

It was time to stop the stupid ego - I really could see it for what it was. Believe me - I wanted to volunteer but was also aware of selfish ambition that I might be making great inroads in 'proving myself' but adding to the historical climate of fear and mistrust brewing up in certain theatres of conflict. I really did - Dammit! And I wanted to do this.

So a teacher I am; no real stories of daring-do, no real bravado, no real status, but you're an idiot if you think I just got cold feet. I've had to take the cynical remarks and the senseless opinions of non-combatants and (less so) combatants ever since; I still did my bit to the best of my ability - it took sacrifice and skill.

So I enrolled on an 'A' level course whilst at the same time taking my expensive Airline exams and having a fleeting one month relationship with a fellow Airwoman that blew my mind and made me realise, through a therapist, that I needed to take a few risks. But there was a problem. I'm not all that clever, my A levels weren't that good even though I loved the subject of Literature. Yeah, that's right – that's how hard I have to work to get anywhere, it's also one of the reasons I wanted to teach - I'd had to struggle so could sympathise and perhaps help - I excitedly took delivery of my A level re-take kit like some enthusiastic skinny bloke who's ordered a bull worker through the mail order comic and expects to be Charles Atlas in two weeks, I discovered that I'd improved over the years - something had clicked, and I thought I could explain all this to students like me who were struggling.

It didn't look much, a plastic folder with twenty booklets telling me what to do, I was assured there was a respectable teacher somewhere in Islington ready to mark my work and give advice whilst I agonized over my essays; how many times had I submitted such painstaking work all those years back to my excellent English teacher, only to receive a dismissive 'E' at the top each time.

But this time they said 'B' or even high 'B', I think there might have been the odd 'A'. I have no idea what I was doing differently. Bristol University asked me to compare two poems as an entry test and said if I got a 'B' or above I was in.

My English teacher had been funny, opinionated, committed, above all it was the only time when I had genuinely heard reasoned debate about important moral questions with opposing views rather than one right wing conservative versus another. It was where I'd read stuff that began to make sense in this military world. The ethical choices of Hamlet, the Wasteland of TS Eliot, the timeless waiting of Godot - it all came clear now and I thought perhaps that is where I should be setting my sights – but without a weapon. I wasn't that good at English but I loved it, loved the effect it had; best of all, I felt it was a worthwhile pursuit. There was no doubt it was a good thing to do. Whether I could do it was another question.

I'm not a great fan of Bono's music, but I think he'd be pleased to know the effect he'd had. He and my English teacher. I was clearly going to be bloody useless hemmed up in a classroom, but so what, at least I wasn't killing anyone.

The irony is, the people I work with now are a sort of elite of their own making. Dedication, skill under pressure, relentless devotion to duty, sudden inspired moments in which impressive things occur. All the qualities I was in search of all those years ago on II Squadron, here they are in the staff room; and yet they are the most criticised, most under pressure, most ignored group I've come across. There's no great initiation test, just hanging in there during the PGCE facing a new class every day; no balloon jump, just Monday morning.

I remember thinking , as I left the RAF, I'd be back in Bath teaching as soon as possible after my degree, put down a deposit on a flat, girlfriend (of the time) would move in. But I took a leap and went to London to do drama school, lost the deposit on the course, lost the girlfriend, didn't move back to Bath. But I managed to hang on to my old friends. I'm not sure I agree with what the RAF has done since but it's none of my business; no one wants to kill anyone either so I find it hard to recommend; but in terms of teamwork, experience, escape, opportunity to meet some great people I end up sounding like a bloody careers brochure. So people get confused when they meet me and find a left-leaning pacifist who fought for his country and is moved to tears when talking of the RAF and the great people I met there.

Since that time I've moved to Bristol, scene of my University days, and teach English and Film to 16-19 year olds. Oh and I'm trying to write, so thanks for reading.

Chapter 48

Final thoughts

I knew what I'd do; sitting in the Psychotherapist's chair just after my fleeting one month affair; I realised that I needed to take a few risks; I'd already put in for premature voluntary release because the RAF were offering them - if I got out now I could grow my hair long, become an ecologically-living leftie who wandered about in an old army jacket hanging about University lectures and then start teaching, live in a Georgian house in Bath stacked high with books, wearing tweed and throwing out quotes of TS Eliot and Oscar Wilde at the drop of a panama hat - they always had stable families with wine and literary parties. It was so far away it seemed wonderful and in a never-never land. It was hard enough trying to become a pilot; surely a degree followed by making it as a teacher? Very unlikely...but I discovered, start walking and it's like that Volcano in Mexico...

After fifteen years of dedicated and single-minded devotion to duty I was still a Co-pilot, I'd met one woman who'd ditched me after a month, and now this one had done the same. It hadn't been the world of sports cars and womanising the 1960s films and posters had been promising and I'd been expecting; whilst I'd been to countless weddings performing the guard of honour, I'd personally led a monastic existence completely committed to surviving in my job and personal fitness - and wasn't anywhere becoming 'human' in my view; I needed to get out and be a part of the community, it may not suit me but I needed to try.

Maybe then I'd become the average married man with kids and all the usual trappings... but I was attracted to risk in choice of partners - hence the fleeting relationships - maybe I needed to find it within myself.

I questioned our role in Ireland, I questioned our role in Iraq and how much good it did, I questioned whether flying airlines was indeed the bravest thing I could do - or just a continuation of exactly what I'd been doing all these years and meeting no social group, had no attractive female friends, no crew cut blonde haired women like you see in the Tank Girl comics or playing guitar in Roxette. I wasn't living, and it didn't hinge around money. I felt jealous of those Doc Martin wearing blokes hanging out with women who had quiffs and wore braces and probably voted labour. Heck, there was another life out there but I was far too square, militaristic, right wing and interested in planes to meet such people...wasn't I?

Even though the RAF would give me a hefty package of £46,000 and a pension, by leaving early I was losing about eighty grand in wages. But I wanted to psychologically make that leap; I took my airline exams and re-took my shoddy English 'A' level (Bristol University made me compare two poems as an essay, then offered me a place if I got a 'B' in English Lit'); I remember, sat in the corner of Queen's Square, Bath; I opened the thin envelope, the blue print flapped in the light August breeze as the cars drove round the light brown Georgian buildings. Would I make this first step into the world of 'Art'? Would they allow me in? I followed the dotted line of the small print - checked my name and let my eyes rest on...English Literature.... my then girlfriend hugged me, a new window had opened, a new world awaited. I was going to grow my hair long, live for poetry and discard my past. I would write journalism, epic novels, shine a light on the world of conflict... let's face it I was being slightly naive - it was only a 'B'.

Very surprisingly I was allowed in to the world of University students and welcomed by what I thought would be hostile teenagers, but instead were charming, open minded and of staggeringly ability - as the coming years demonstrated; I was welcomed onto teacher training because they needed teachers; there were no 'wings' - no 'wall' barring you from joining the big boys club... but it was definitely hard - in some ways harder than fast jet selection, because you leave of your own volition - no need to kick you out; if you're not getting through the pupils let you know it, life is unbearable and you leave of your own accord. But somehow I just kept making myself turn up. Despite a class with no door, my predecessor committing suicide and at one stage the school running out of paper.

But in the midst of University I'd discovered acting - it's a book for another time - but I had to get this out of my system and enrolled at East 15 drama school; the most sure-fire way of breaking every personal behaviour barrier of my own, finding the coolest friends I'd never normally meet in this lifetime and having some of the most outrageous stories to tell - and all without the need for conflict. Whilst rehearsing with East 15 I witnessed teamwork, professional commitment and the sorts of things I'd seen in the RAF, but these guys had no jobs to go to! They just wanted to do it and had no thought of tomorrow, driven by that urge to do something spectacular, for other people's enjoyment; it 's a noble art, it really is. I just couldn't pay the rent and I know that doesn't stop those great people I've met on the way, but hey, maybe that world was beginning to let me in after all. Suddenly. On my fortieth I'm surrounded by actors, performers, dancers and throwing myself about in the very pub they filmed Withnail (film) before turning it into something else. It was fleeting, but then - I enjoyed whilst I could.

So I got a job in a school for a year, in a class without a door, some days without paper, following on from suicides and teachers who lasted two weeks. I spent a year there and looked elsewhere, thankfully, after happily riding about London as a courier whilst attempting to survive as an actor, I was rung by a friend of a fellow English teacher - June - eventual Phd and emigre to Grenada; but at that moment, luckily for me, a Further Education College Head of English and she told me this was more my world - A levels - what I'd always been aiming for. Thank you June. I miss acting, miss flying, miss running (colitis), most of all miss the people I met whilst doing these things; mercifully I've stayed in touch with a lot of these stars - and that's the best reward, success, prize of all. Through the losses I guess I've better realised how to appreciate those that I now meet on the way.

I now cycle to work - which is a Bristol sixth form college, frantically teach 'A' level literature, film, and GCSEs and also run the debating society with a pupil. I struggle at it but it's a learning curve. As always with anything it seems, I work very hard to achieve 'average'. But I have a rented ground floor Georgian flat, practice a keyboard on which I've learnt three songs to impress a casual listener and try to write in the evenings. It's very regular, like clockwork, quite tedious, badly paid and I'm not a natural - I have to work very hard to achieve reasonable. But I'm trying. All these things I've never experienced before and I'm still glad I left, despite the weary look of the pupil who doesn't believe me when I say I was a pilot. To them I'm just that chap in the shirt and tie and it's a humbling experience to walk into a party, someone asks you what you do and you can't say 'Pilot' anymore; instead you say 'teacher' and watch their eyes glaze over, with a swift change of subject. But on the way I've met singers, sculptors, photographers, dancers, actors, directors, comedians, writers, producers; I've hung out with them when they were students, done shows with them, been staggered by their work ethic, discipline, devotion to task, love of life. None of them would I have met, if I hadn't made this leap.

Now I don't come home and immediately start working on how I'd like to be working somewhere else; before I would either be running, working on the airline exam or writing an essay and preparing for University. Now, I have no need to find something that feels like I'm helping the world rather than attacking it, the only person I'm in an argument with isn't a middle eastern despot but a seventeen year-old slacker who thinks the world is going to arrive on a plate; it's a better place.